Pension Markets in Focus 2023

OECD
BETTER POLICIES FOR BETTER LIVES

Please cite this publication as:
OECD (2023), *Pension Markets in Focus 2023*, OECD Publishing, Paris, https://doi.org/10.1787/28970baf-en.

ISBN 978-92-64-44423-2 (print)
ISBN 978-92-64-32204-2 (pdf)
ISBN 978-92-64-39041-6 (HTML)
ISBN 978-92-64-89741-0 (epub)

Photo credits: Cover © grapestock/Adobe Stock

Corrigenda to OECD publications may be found on line at: www.oecd.org/about/publishing/corrigenda.htm.

Foreword

Pension Markets in Focus provides detailed and comparable statistics on asset-backed pension systems around the world. Published annually, the report aims to help policy makers, regulators and other stakeholders evaluate the design and operation of pension systems, and to support policy discussions through international comparisons.

This edition looks at the impact of elevated inflation, higher interest rates and other macro-economic and financial developments on asset-backed pension systems in 2022, and in particular on investment performance, portfolio allocation, participation in pension plans and contributions paid to these plans. The report also examines the evolution of the value of assets earmarked for retirement, the liabilities of defined benefit plans embedding a promise to plan members by plan sponsors, and the fees charged to members of defined contribution plans.

Data used to prepare this report were collected from pension authorities and other bodies within the framework of the OECD's Global Pension Statistics project of the OECD Working Party on Private Pensions. The OECD's partnership with the International Organisation of Pension Supervisors (IOPS) and the World Bank expands the geographical coverage of the report beyond the OECD area. The OECD is grateful to the IOPS and the World Bank who helped in the data collection, and to pension authorities and other reporting bodies for providing data and comments.

The report was prepared by the OECD Directorate for Financial and Enterprise Affairs (DAF) under the leadership of Carmine Di Noia, Director for Financial and Enterprise Affairs, and under the direction of Pablo Antolin, Head of the Insurance and Pensions Unit. This report was prepared by Romain Despalins with inputs from Stéphanie Payet from DAF's Insurance and Pensions Unit. The report benefitted from comments by Serdar Çelik, Head of DAF's Capital Markets and Financial Institutions Division, and Jessica Mosher. Sally Day-Hanotiaux provided statistical assistance. Eva Abbott, Meral Gedik and Flora Monsaingeon-Lavuri provided editorial assistance and prepared for publication.

Table of contents

FIGURES

TABLES

Executive summary

This edition of Pension Markets in Focus examines the effect that elevated inflation, rising interest rates and strong labour markets had on asset-backed pension systems in 2022. It focuses on the impact on investment performance, portfolio allocation, contributions and the evolution of assets earmarked for retirement.

Higher interest rates and falling equity valuations led to widespread investment losses in 2022

The simultaneous fall in bond and equity prices, the two main instruments in portfolios earmarked for retirement, led to widespread nominal investment losses. High inflation rates exacerbated these dynamics, with negative real rates of return observed in most countries. The strong valuation gains achieved in previous years cushioned the impact of these negative rates of return on the long-term investment performance of asset-backed pension systems.

Higher employment rates and nominal wages contributed to a rise in the number of people participating in pension plans and in contributions

Employment rates improved in 2022, with a consequent increase in the proportion of the working-age population covered by a pension plan. This is particularly visible for pension plans that mandate workers' participation. In combination with rising nominal wages, this increase contributed to an overall rise in nominal contributions to pension plans in most jurisdictions. At the same time, in voluntary systems, high inflation may have reduced the ability of some individuals to save for retirement.

Investment losses led to a decline in the value of assets earmarked for retirement in most OECD countries, whereas in several non-OECD jurisdictions this was offset by the surplus of contributions over benefit payments

The positive impact of higher contributions was insufficient to offset the negative impact of investment losses in many OECD countries, leading to a decline in the value of assets earmarked for retirement. However, in several non-OECD jurisdictions, the surplus of contributions over benefit payments offset investment losses, primarily driven by the fact that benefits are still low in many of these jurisdictions where the pay-out phase has not yet, or very recently, started.

The increase in interest rates led to an improvement in the sustainability of defined benefit pension plans in some countries, despite asset valuation decreases

The increase in interest rates has translated into higher discount rates used to calculate the liabilities of defined benefit pension plans, leading to a reduction in the present value of these liabilities. In some countries, the value of liabilities fell more than that of assets, resulting in an improvement in the sustainability of the benefit promise. However, jurisdictions that value liabilities using a fixed discount rate saw a deterioration of the ratio of assets over liabilities.

The effect of developments in 2022 on fees varied depending on the fee structure

Pension providers charge fees to members of defined contribution pension plans to cover the costs of the services they offer. Fees may be levied on contributions, assets or investment performance. The amount of fees collected on contributions generally increases in line with contributions. Fees on assets tend to evolve with the value of assets. The low investment performance in 2022 led to a decline in performance fees.

1 Elevated inflation and rising interest rates led to widespread investment losses

Higher inflation and interest rates characterise the year 2022. The rise in interest rates led to widespread investment losses for asset-backed pension systems in nominal terms. After accounting for high inflation, losses were much larger in real terms. Investment gains in the previous years helped to compensate for the losses over the longer term.

This section examines the impact of elevated inflation and rising interest rates on the rates of return of asset-backed pension systems and their asset allocation. Asset-backed pension systems cover both pension plans that individuals access via their employer or a financial institution and where they accumulate assets or rights (hereafter 'pension plans') and public reserves that social security institutions or governments build up to support public unfunded or pay-as-you-go systems, and which are generally held separately in ring-fenced funds (hereafter 'public pension reserve funds').[1]

1.1. Asset-backed pension systems suffered investment losses on several asset classes simultaneously

Assets earmarked for retirement are mainly invested in bonds and equities. These two instruments accounted for more than 70% of the investments of pension plans and close to 90% for public pension reserve funds on average at end-2021, with an asset mix varying across jurisdictions (Figure 1.1). Those favouring bonds, in particular government bonds, may do so due to the perceived income stability and the lower risk level of these instruments compared to others, a lack of other investment opportunities domestically, the existence of guarantees or a recent introduction of pension plans.[2] In some cases, regulation may also require a minimum proportion of assets to be invested in bonds (e.g. those with a multi-fund structure with floors (OECD, 2023[1])) or all in bonds (e.g. the US Old-Age and Survivors Insurance Trust Fund that is required by law to invest fully in non-marketable US government bonds). Those with higher allocations to equities may have been seeking higher returns by taking more risks, such as the Japan's Government Pension Investment Fund and Korea's National Pension Fund.

Figure 1.1. Allocation of assets earmarked for retirement in selected asset classes and investment vehicles, at end-2021

As a percentage of total investment

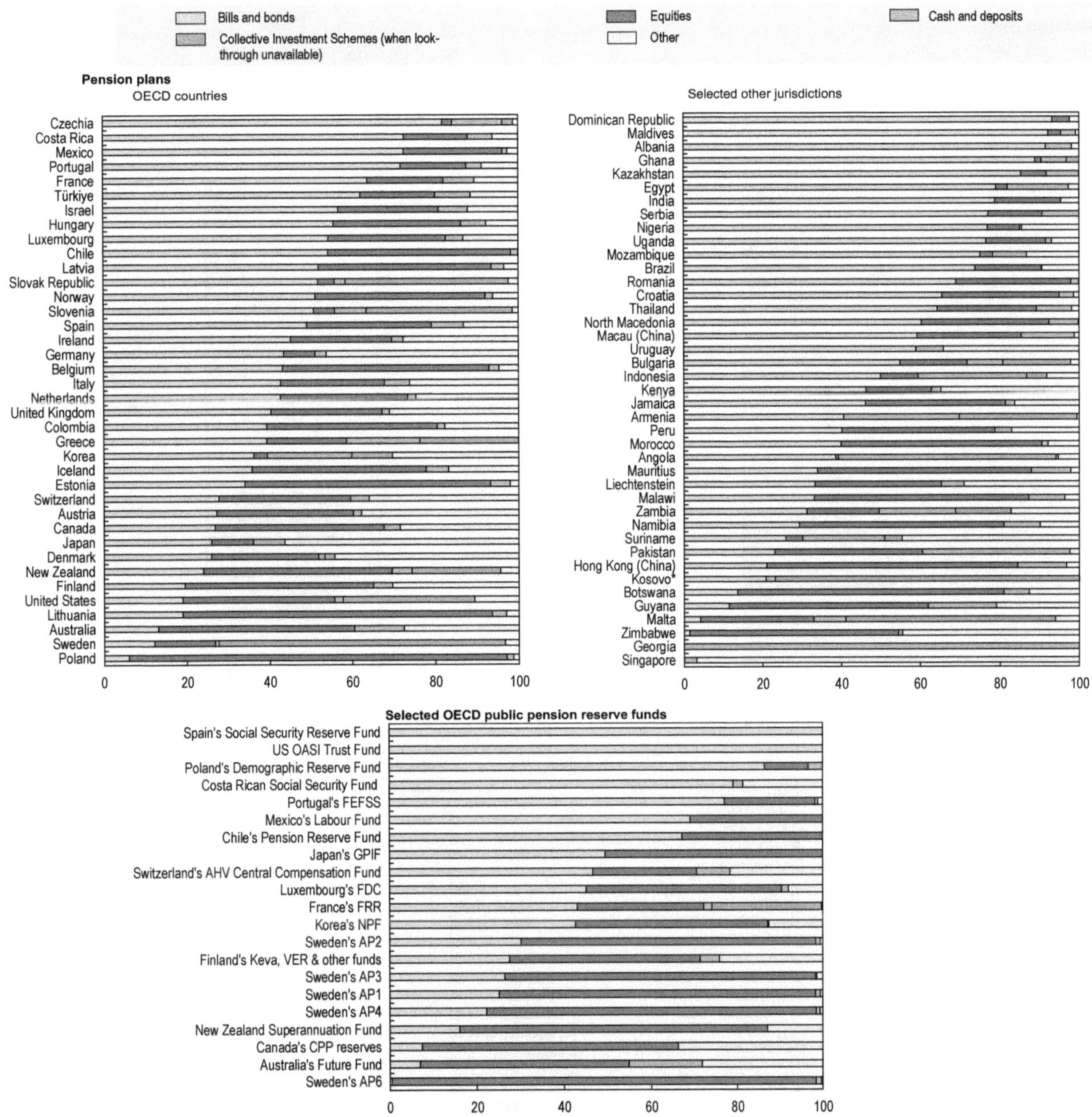

Note: For more details, please see the methodological notes in Annex C.

* This designation is without prejudice to positions on status, and is in line with United Nations Security Council Resolution 1244/99 and the Advisory Opinion of the International Court of Justice on Kosovo's declaration of independence.

Source: OECD Global Pension Statistics and other sources.

StatLink https://stat.link/7dv6ka

Asset-backed pension systems were hit by the simultaneous fall in bond and equity prices in 2022. The rise in interest rates lowered the value of bonds in pension investment portfolios. At the same time, equity markets also fell globally, with prices down by 19% for S&P500, by 9% for Nikkei 225 and by 12% for DAX at end-2022 compared to end-2021 for example.[3] Pension plans and public pension reserve funds incurred losses both on their bond and equity holdings, resulting in overall negative rates of return in nominal terms in many jurisdictions in 2022 (Figure 1.2).

Figure 1.2. Nominal and real investment rates of return (IRR) of asset-backed pension systems, Dec 2021 - Dec 2022

In per cent

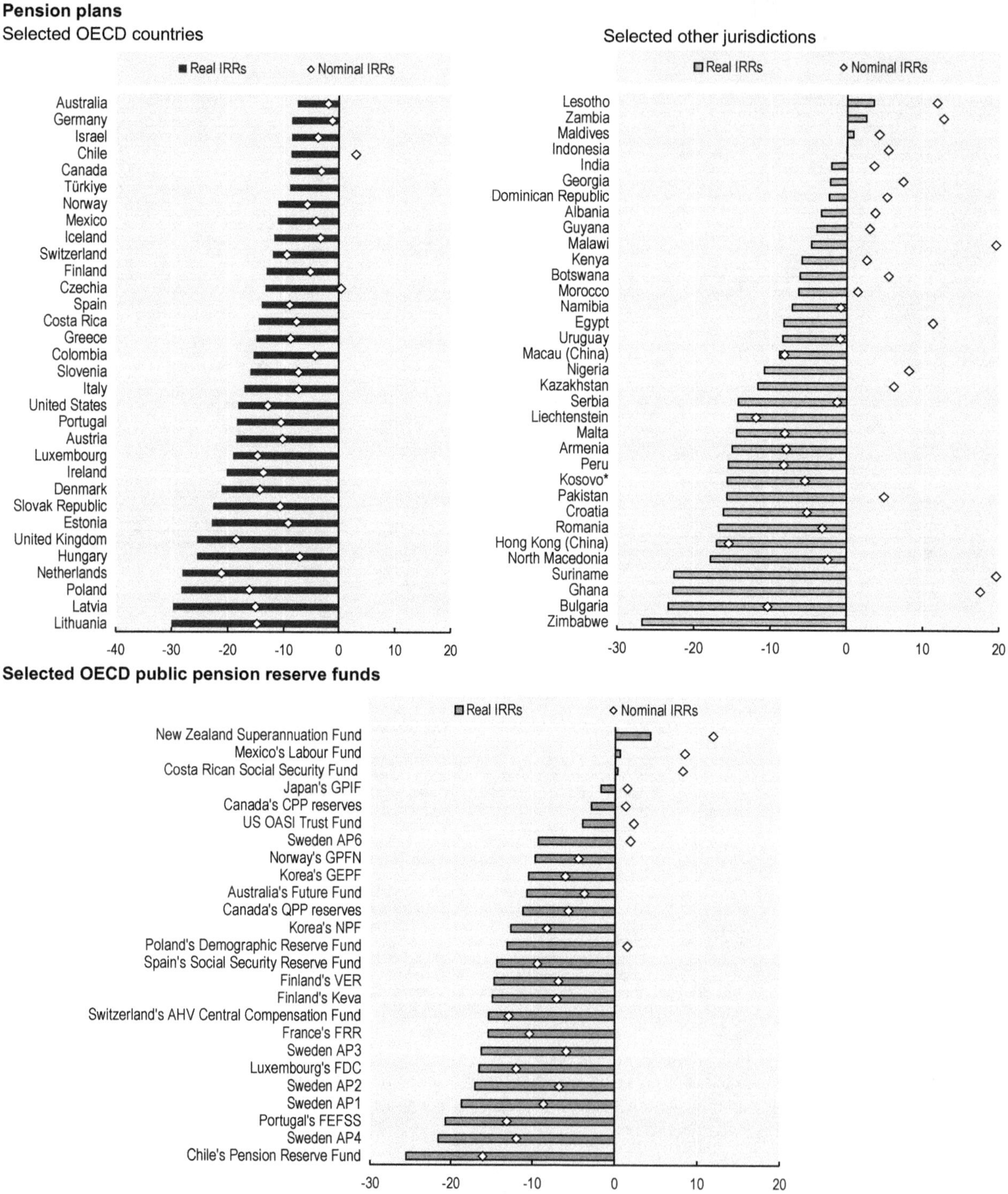

Note: For more details, please see the methodological notes in Annex C.
Source: OECD Global Pension Statistics and other sources.

StatLink https://stat.link/ofjg64

In addition to equity and bond portfolios, losses on other financial instruments also contributed to negative nominal returns. In a context of rising interest rates, pension plans in the Netherlands and the United Kingdom suffered losses on their interest-rate derivatives held to hedge against the risk of declining interest rates. Dutch pension funds also recorded losses on their real estate investments.[4] These losses, combined with those on bonds and equities, led pension plans in the Netherlands and the United Kingdom to record the lowest nominal returns among all reporting jurisdictions (-21.1% and -18.5% respectively).

Meanwhile, pension plans in some countries benefitted from the changes in foreign exchange rates. The rapid rise in interest rates in the United States made US dollars attractive to investors, who sold other currencies to purchase them, which strengthened the US dollar against these other currencies (Alderman, Camp and Mandiak, 2023[2]). Some pension plans achieved foreign exchange gains on their investments abroad, as the domestic currency depreciated against the US dollar (e.g. the Netherlands). These gains offset some of the investment losses and even resulted in positive investment rates of return in some countries (e.g. Zambia).

The method of valuing assets can influence the investment performance results. For instance, the rise in interest rates in domestic government bonds had little effect on the value of bond holdings when pension funds value assets following an amortised cost method based on effective interest rates (e.g. Albania). Similarly, since early 2022, the Demographic Reserve Fund in Poland has also been valuing its debt securities according to the adjusted purchase price determined based on the effective interest rate, as the reserve fund intends to hold its debt securities until maturity. This valuation method does not capture the decline in the price of debt instruments following interest rate hikes in the performance results.

Elevated inflation turned nominal investment gains into real losses and made nominal losses much larger in real terms. Real rates of return were negative for pension plans in all OECD countries and nearly all reporting non-OECD jurisdictions. Real rates of return were the lowest in some of the countries where inflation surged the most (e.g. Hungary, Latvia and Lithuania with annual rates over 20% in December 2022 (OECD, 2023[3]) among OECD countries, and Ghana, Suriname and Zimbabwe outside the OECD, where the consumer price index rose by 52%, 55% and 111% respectively). Most public pension reserve funds also experienced real losses in 2022. Real rates of return were positive in 2022 in just a couple of African countries (Lesotho, Zambia) and the Maldives, where inflation did not offset nominal investment gains.[5]

Strong investment gains in the previous years helped to compensate for the losses in 2022 in many jurisdictions. Pension plans reached an average annual return above inflation in 21 out of 55 reporting jurisdictions (i.e. in 38% of the reporting jurisdictions) over the last 5 years, 33 out of 44 (i.e. 75%) over the last 10 years, 24 out 34 (i.e. 71%) over the last 15 years, and 15 out of 19 (i.e. 79%) over the last 20 years (Table 1.1). The investment performance of public pension reserve funds was also positive in real terms over the last 15 or 20 years in all those for which data are available.

Table 1.1. Geometric average annual real investment rates over the last 5, 10, 15 and 20 years

In per cent

Pension plans

Selected OECD countries	5-yr average	10-yr average	15-yr average	20-yr average
Australia	3.3	5.4	2.8	4.0
Austria	-2.9	0.2	-0.3	0.8
Canada	1.7	3.9	3.6	4.1
Chile	0.1	2.0	1.4	3.1
Colombia	0.2	1.4	3.8	4.8
Costa Rica	3.8	5.1	3.7	..
Czechia	-4.7	-2.4	-1.7	-1.0
Denmark	-0.8	1.9	2.6	3.3
Estonia	-4.1	-1.0	-2.2	-1.1
Finland	1.6	3.6	..	..
Germany	-0.6	1.2	1.6	1.9
Greece	-0.7	..	..	..
Hungary	-6.3	-0.3	..	..
Iceland	3.6	4.2	1.7	3.3
Ireland	1.1	..	..	..
Israel	3.5	4.7	3.8	..
Italy	-2.5	0.2	0.3	0.9
Latvia	-6.3	-2.2	-1.8	-1.9
Lithuania	-4.6	-0.5	..	..
Luxembourg	-3.2	-0.2	-0.2	..
Mexico	0.3	0.5	1.4	..
Netherlands	-3.2	1.3	1.8	3.1
Norway	0.2	2.4	2.2	3.5
Poland	-7.2	..	..	..
Portugal	-1.8	0.8	0.0	1.6
Slovak Republic	-4.4	-1.4	-1.7	..
Slovenia	-2.6	1.2	2.0	..
Spain	-1.8	1.1	0.6	..
Switzerland	0.8	2.9	2.3	2.8
Türkiye	-3.5	-2.2	-0.3	..
United States	-1.4	1.4	-0.1	1.0

Selected other jurisdictions	5-yr average	10-yr average	15-yr average	20-yr average
Albania	0.7	2.0	2.7	..
Armenia	0.1	..	..	..
Botswana	0.6	..	..	..
Bulgaria	-5.8	-0.7	-2.2	-0.8
Croatia	-1.6	..	..	..
Dominican Republic	3.3	5.8	6.3	..
Egypt	2.4	..	..	..
Guyana	-0.9	..	..	..
Hong Kong (China)	-2.6	-0.1	..	..
Indonesia	3.3	3.6	..	..
Kazakhstan	-0.4	..	..	..
Kosovo*	-2.4	1.2	..	..
Liechtenstein	-0.4	2.6	1.7	..
Malawi	3.5	3.4	..	..
Maldives	4.4	4.9	..	..
Nigeria	-4.0	-2.2	..	..
North Macedonia	-0.7	2.4	1.9	..
Pakistan	-6.0	..	..	..
Peru	-1.7	0.3	0.1	3.3
Romania	-2.1	1.6	..	..
Serbia	-1.8	2.9	1.1	..
Suriname	-14.5	..	..	..
Uruguay	-0.2	2.1	3.9	..
Zambia	0.1	2.4	3.0	..

Selected OECD public pension reserve funds

Selected reserve funds	5-yr average	10-yr average	15-yr average	20-yr average
Australia's Future Fund	3.9	6.3	4.9	..
Canada's CPP reserves	4.6	7.4	5.7	6.5
Canada's QPP reserves	2.5	6.0	..	..
Chile's Pension Reserve F	1.5	2.9	2.2	..
Finland's Keva	1.3	3.9	2.9	..
Finland's VER	1.1	3.4	2.7	3.8
France's FRR	-2.1	1.5	0.5	..
Japan's GPIF	4.1	4.4	3.9	3.9
Korea's GEPF	1.7	..	..	..
Korea's NPF	1.9	2.9	2.9	..
Luxembourg's FDC	0.2	2.5	2.3	..
New Zealand Superannua	4.8	8.6	7.2	7.2
Norway's GPFN	2.3	5.2	4.3	5.6
Poland's Demographic Re	-5.0	-1.3	-0.6	1.3
Spain's Social Security Re	-4.7	-0.4	0.4	0.3
Sweden AP1	2.6	5.7	4.2	..
Sweden AP2	1.1	5.0	3.7	5.6
Sweden AP3	3.9	6.8	4.7	..
Sweden AP4	2.8	6.7	5.2	6.3
Sweden AP6	12.2	10.4	6.6	7.3
Switzerland's AHV Centra	-0.8	2.1	..	..
US OASI Trust Fund	-1.1	0.4	1.2	1.5

Note: For more details, please see the methodological notes in Annex C.
Source: OECD Global Pension Statistics and other sources.

StatLink https://stat.link/2fsltz

Countries where pension plans failed to generate a positive cumulative return above inflation over the past 20-year period invested conservatively. Bulgaria, Czechia, Estonia and Latvia all have negative average annual real rates of return and high bond proportions in their pension investment portfolios (Figure 1.1).[6]

1.2. Elevated inflation and rising interest rates may have spurred a change in asset allocation

The proportion of pension assets invested in equities dropped in most countries in 2022 (Figure 1.3). This could be the result of the fall in equity prices, but also of a decision to move away from equities in a global context of uncertainty with high inflation, volatility in equity markets and fears of recession.[7] This fall in equity holdings occurred even in some countries that changed their default investment strategies to encourage more risk-taking to achieve higher long-term returns (e.g. Croatia, Lithuania and New Zealand).[8] Yet some other countries that also encouraged more risk taking during the accumulation phase increased their equity allocations despite the decline in equity valuations, such as Estonia.[9]

Figure 1.3. Variation in the proportion of pension assets invested in bonds and equities between end-2021 and end-2022 in selected OECD and non-OECD jurisdictions

In percentage points

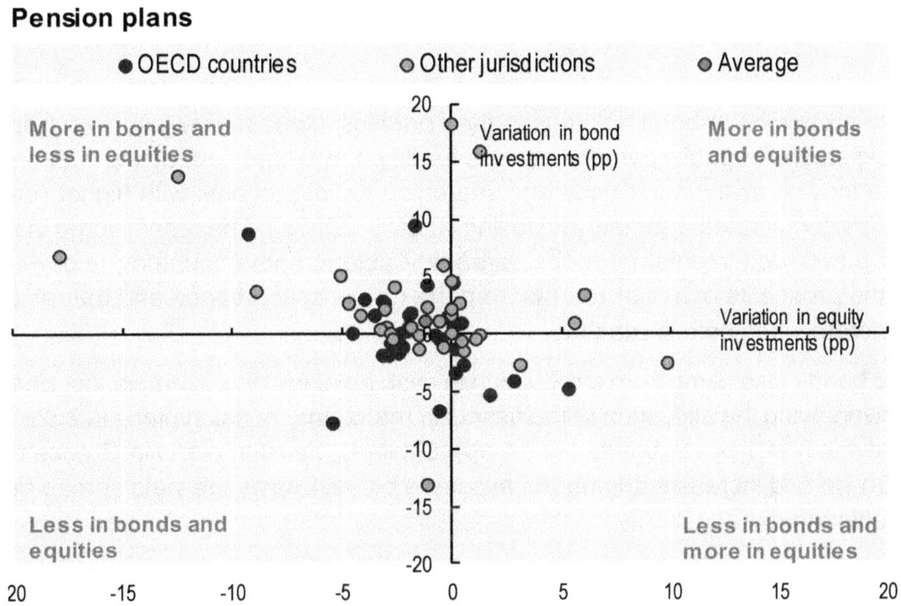

Selected OECD public pension reserve funds

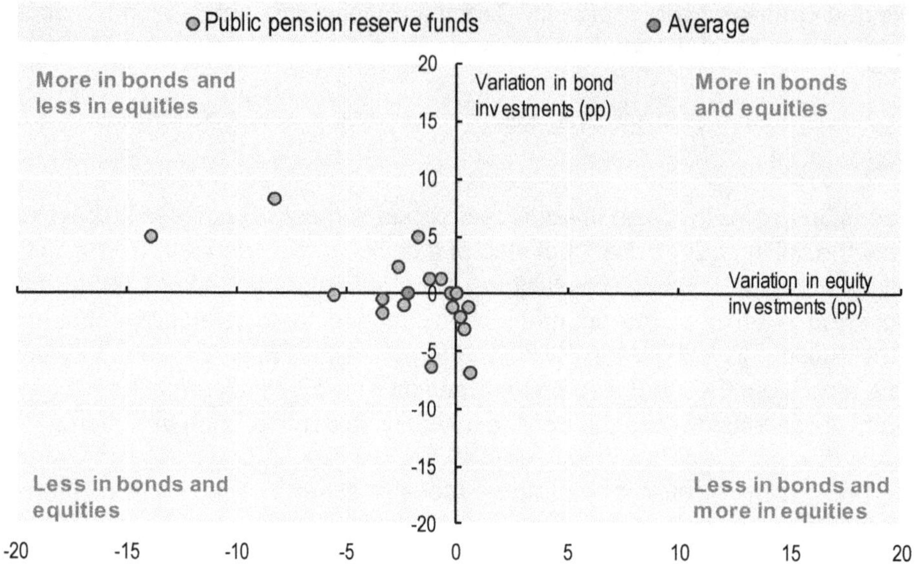

Note: For more details, please see the methodological notes in Annex C.
Source: OECD Global Pension Statistics.

StatLink https://stat.link/5wkl76

Bonds may have benefitted to some extent from this shift away from equities. Although their prices also declined in 2022, the proportion of bond holdings in the portfolios increased by just over 1 pp for pension plans while remaining stable for public pension reserve funds on average, contrasting with previous years when investors were moving away from bonds and searching for instruments with higher return potential (including equities) as interest rates were low and falling (OECD, 2023[4]). The recent surge in interest rates may have triggered a renewed interest in bonds, already visible in some countries (e.g. +4 pp in North Macedonia), given the prospects of higher returns from the newly issued bonds and the relative safety of the income they generate when held to maturity.

Higher allocations to bonds also came from a reduction in cash holdings. For example, the pension agency in Georgia started diversifying the allocation of the assets in mandatory pension plans in 2022 and diverted most of its cash holdings (-34.7 pp) to bonds (+27.4 pp). Similarly, pension plans in Greece reduced their cash holdings by 10.1 pp and increased their bond exposure by +9.4 pp as the yield spread between cash and bonds was broadening.

At the same time, in several reporting jurisdictions pension plans increased their cash holdings, mainly as a result of pension reforms rather than market developments.[10] In the Slovak Republic, pension funds needed liquidity (+ 8 pp to cash) to carry out the transfer of assets from the bond funds to the new default life cycle pension funds introduced in 2023. In Peru, pension funds also increased their cash holdings (+1.5 pp) to comply with their obligations, should members request early access to their savings as the Congress allowed six times between 2020 and 2022. In the United Kingdom, market developments with the sharp rise in gilt yield in September 2022 led pension plans that use liability-driven investing (LDI) strategies to hedge their liabilities against a decline in interest rates to sell assets to get cash. However, the overall increase in cash holdings of all pension funds was rather limited overall (+0.8 pp at end-2022) probably as a result of the intervention of the Bank of England to cool the gilt market.[11] The increase in cash holdings of pension plans was more substantial in the Netherlands (e.g. + 1.3 pp) to meet margin calls from interest-rate derivatives. However, pension funds had margin call related activities (such as derivatives and repurchase agreements) in less than half of IOPS reporting Members (14 out of 37 reporting jurisdictions) and faced no significant liquidity risk arising from margin calls according to their pension supervisors (Oh and Stańko, 2023[5]).

The proportion of assets invested in other instruments than equities, bonds and cash (hereafter 'alternative investments') also increased for pension plans and public pension reserve funds in most reporting jurisdictions in 2022.[12] Some of these alternative investments generated positive investment income (e.g. private equity in Colombia), while others (e.g. direct real estate in the Netherlands and Switzerland) recorded lower losses than traditional instruments and other alternative instruments that are more sensitive to market fluctuations (e.g. securitised debt).[13] While alternative investments benefitted from the search for yield during the period of low and falling interest rates, some may continue to attract asset managers for their capacity to hedge against inflation (such as in Asia).[14] Some jurisdictions have also been promoting alternative investments by pension plans by removing or lifting barriers in investment regulations (e.g. Colombia).[15] Several public pension reserve funds also increased their alternative investments, with the largest rise for the New Zealand Superannuation Fund (by 9 pp between June 2021 and June 2022) driven by an increased allocation to infrastructure, property and other alternatives.[16]

Notes

[1] See Annex A for a more detailed description of asset-backed pension systems and their features.

[2] The lack of depth and breadth of local capital markets may have contributed to the large allocation of assets to public debt in some Latin American countries (e.g. Costa Rica, Dominican Republic and Uruguay) (Mesa-Lago, 2020[14]). Pension plans introduced earlier (e.g. Chile) may have a more diversified strategy than others in Latin America (FIAP, 2018[15]).

[3] Market Data (wsj.com)

[4] Pension funds suffer losses on real estate (dnb.nl)

[5] The Maldives benefitted from the recovery of the domestic economy following the rebound of tourism in 2022.

[6] In Estonia, the lifting of ceiling on equities has led to a surge in the proportion of assets invested in equities (from 34% in 2018 to 64% in 2022) and a decline in the proportion invested in bonds (from 62% in 2018 to 29% in 2022). This recent move to more risky investment has not yet led to positive long-term returns due to the downturn in equity markets in 2022 and the lack of a sufficient number of more buoyant years.

[7] Some of these equity investments were carried out abroad, which may also explain some of the decline in foreign investments (e.g. Chile). See the statistical annex for the evolution of foreign investments (Annex B).

[8] Croatia and New Zealand changed their default investment strategy to a less conservative one in 2019 and 2021 respectively. Lithuania established life-cycle funds as the default option in 2019.

[9] Estonia raised the limit to invest in equities from 75% to 100% in 2019 for non-conservative funds.

[10] With respect to public pension reserve funds in the OECD, cash holdings declined in half of them.

[11] The limited movement in cash may also be related to a deleveraging strategy from UK pension funds in the last quarter of 2022, where more liquid assets were likely used to pay down relating to repurchase agreements (Office for National Statistics, 2023[17]).

[12] The proportion of assets in other investments than equities, bonds, and cash (and collective investment schemes when the look-through is not available) increased in 30 out of 35 reporting OECD countries, 27 out of 38 reporting non-OECD jurisdictions and 12 out of 20 selected OECD public pension reserve funds. See statistical annex for the evolution of the asset allocation of pension plans over the years (Annex B).

[13] Pension funds suffer losses on real estate (dnb.nl) and Compenswiss holds strategy as first pillar reform gives room for illiquid investments | News | IPE

[14] Asia's Pension Funds Allocate Further to Alternatives | Cerulli

[15] Colombia issued a Decree in 2022 removing all the limits on alternative investments that were set before and requiring a minimum investment in private equity or private debt.

[16] NZ Super Fund - Annual Report

2 Higher nominal wages and employment rates contributed to a rise in contributions

The amount of assets accumulated depends on the investment income earned as well as the amount of contributions paid into and outpayments from the pension plans. Developments in labour markets can influence the number of people participating in pension plans and the amount they contribute.

Labour markets have benefited from the economic recovery following the COVID-19 crisis. The proportion of the population employed continued to increase in 2022 globally after a robust employment growth in 2021. At the same time, nominal wages have picked up in a context of rising inflation, although at a slower pace than inflation and with a lag.

These developments in the labour markets explain the rise in nominal contributions. The improvements in employment rates contributed to an increase in the proportion of people participating in pension plans. This increase, in combination with rising nominal wages and various policy measures to encourage people to join and contribute to pension plans, led to a rise in nominal contributions. At the same time, high inflation and the rising cost of living may have discouraged some individuals to save for retirement in voluntary systems and lower the growth rate of contributions.

This section explains how labour market developments and other factors influenced the participation in and contributions to pension plans in 2022.

2.1. Improvements in employment rates contributed to an increase in the proportion of people participating in pension plans

Employment rates have improved since the shock of COVID-19 crisis on labour markets, and their recovery supported the increase in the proportion of the working-age population having a pension plan in 2022. The increase in the participation rate was widespread across jurisdictions and types of plans but was more systematic for plans mandating workers to participate (Figure 2.1).[1] This increase was particularly important in countries that introduced mandatory plans recently (e.g. Armenia, the Dominican Republic, Georgia) and have not reached the entire target population yet.[2] The only country with a decline in participation rate in 2022 among mandatory plans was Estonia, as members have been given the possibility to opt out of the second pension pillar since 2021. The increase in participation was also visible in most countries with automatic enrolment programmes – signing up employees to a plan while granting them the option to opt out – and many countries with voluntary occupational plans, although the increases in participation rates were more limited in these cases.

Figure 2.1. Change in the participation rate in pension plans between 2021 and 2022, by type of plan and by jurisdiction

In percentage point of the working-age population

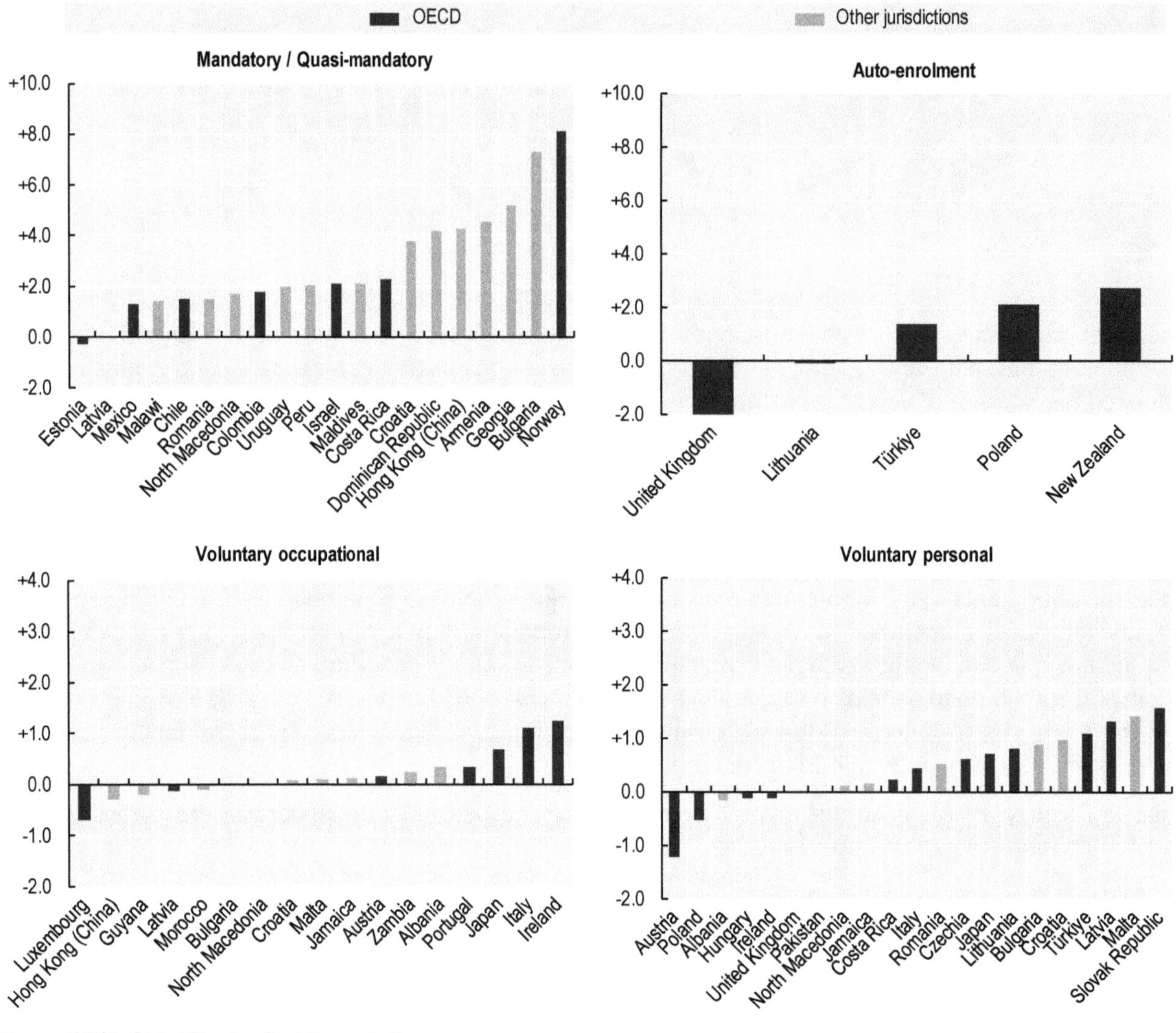

Source: OECD Global Pension Statistics and other sources.

StatLink https://stat.link/1wel3j

The combination of elevated inflation and rising interest rates may have played an opposite effect to the one from the rise of employment rates, discouraging enrolment in a pension plan in some cases when members' participation is voluntary. In the United Kingdom, the participation rate declined for the first time since the introduction of automatic enrolment in 2012, which may be due to an increase in the opt-out rate amid the cost-of-living crisis.[3] At the same time, voluntary plans may have faced competition with other financial products, such as saving products offering higher guaranteed returns in a context of higher interest rates, as reported by the Portuguese pension supervisor. In Austria, the number of personal pension insurance contracts (PZV) continued to decline in 2022, losing popularity since 2012 following a cut in government subsidies for these contracts.

Overall, participation rates continued to increase in 2022, in line with the long-term trend over the past 10 to 20 years,[4] resulting to some extent from the various measures that policy makers have implemented over the years to promote participation in pension plans and diversify the sources to finance retirement. These measures to boost participation rates include the loosening or removal of some eligibility criteria to participate in mandatory plans (e.g. Australia, Norway), the introduction of automatic enrolment programmes (e.g. Lithuania, New Zealand, Poland, Türkiye, the United Kingdom), the introduction of new plans (e.g. People's Republic of China, hereafter 'China') sometimes targeting specific categories of the population through tailored plans (e.g. in several African countries for informal workers), the increase of financial incentives (OECD, 2022[6]), and financial education campaigns. Some of these measures were introduced in 2022 or very recently and had effects already visible by end-2022 (e.g. Norway, the Slovak Republic). In Norway, the coverage of mandatory occupational plans increased by more than 8 pp in 2022 after the expansion of access to all workers earning at least NOK 1 000 from age 13 (instead of 20), including seasonal workers and part-time workers who no longer need to fulfil a minimum of 20% of full-time employment from 1 January 2022. The Slovak Republic recorded the strongest increase in participation rate among voluntary personal plans (+1.6 pp), which may be the result of the recent financial education initiatives set up by the National Bank (*5 peňazí*), together with the communication by the industry on the positive investment returns in 2021.

Despite the general increases in plan participation during 2022, there were still wide differences in the proportion of people having a plan across jurisdictions and types of plans. Mandatory plans and those with an automatic enrolment mechanism are those covering the largest proportion of the working-age population, with a very high or quasi-universal participation rate (Figure 2.2). Participation rates tend to be lower in voluntary plans, with some exceptions such as in Czechia (64%), Ireland (59%), Japan (53%), Poland (65% for open pension funds, formerly mandatory) and the Slovak Republic (48%). Lower participation rates could reflect barriers that may have prevented individuals from joining a plan: eligibility criteria, informality (e.g. in Africa, Asia or Latin America (ILO, 2020[7])), lack of access to an occupational plan because employers are not willing to bear the related costs and administrative burden (OECD, 2022[8]), lack of awareness or appetite from the population.

Figure 2.2. Participation rate in pension plans, by type of plan and jurisdiction, in 2022

As a percentage of the working-age population

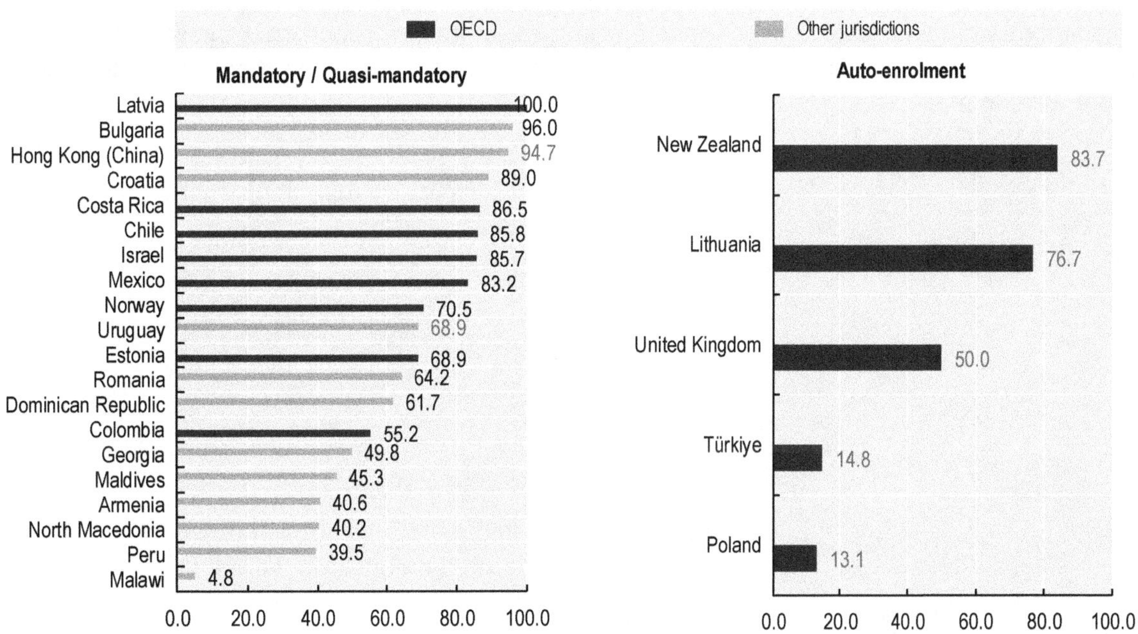

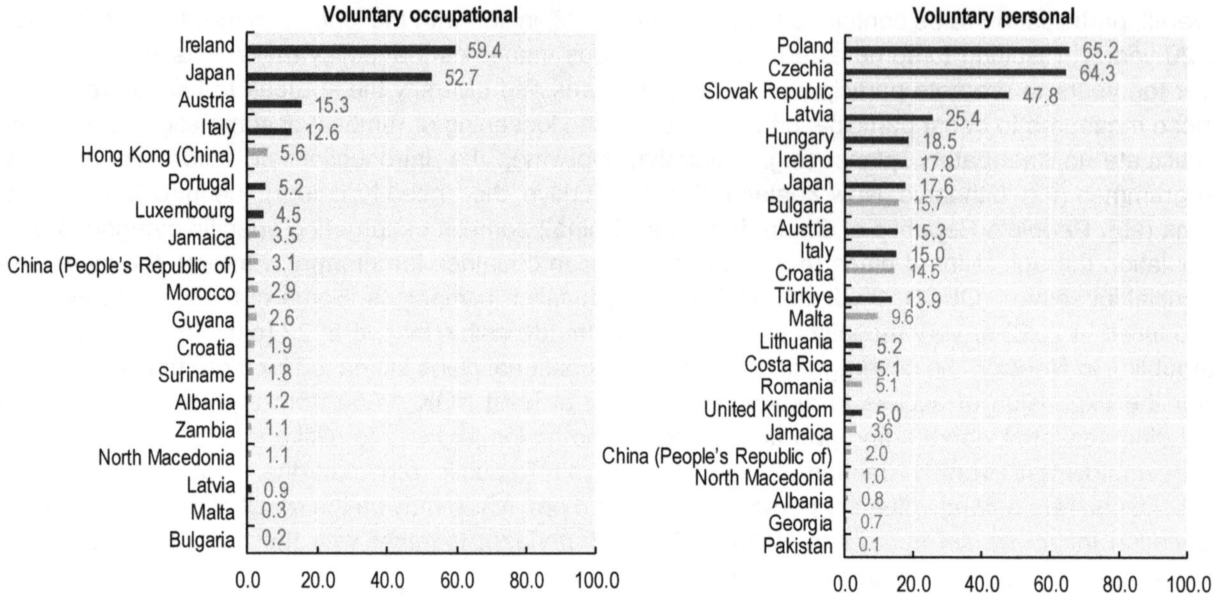

Note: For more details, please see the methodological notes in Annex C.
Source: OECD Global Pension Statistics; Central Statistical Office (Ireland); Ministry of Health, Labour and Welfare (Japan); Finance Norway; DWP's Family Resources Survey (United Kingdom).

StatLink https://stat.link/yvi65h

2.2. Nominal contributions increased as a result of both higher participation and higher nominal wages

Contributions to pension plans increased in most jurisdictions in 2022. Figure 2.3 shows the extent of the increase in nominal contributions across jurisdictions. This increase continued the long-term trend of growing amounts paid into pension plans (OECD, 2023[4]). The increase in participation is one of the factors behind it. However, countries where participation increased the most in 2022 (i.e. Norway and Bulgaria) were not those with the largest rise in contributions, which were Türkiye (69%) and Estonia (64%). Also, contributions increased in 2022 even in some countries where the proportion of the working-age population having a plan stalled or declined (e.g. Estonia, Luxembourg, the United Kingdom), showing that other factors were at play.

Figure 2.3. Nominal growth rate of contributions into pension plans, 2022

In per cent

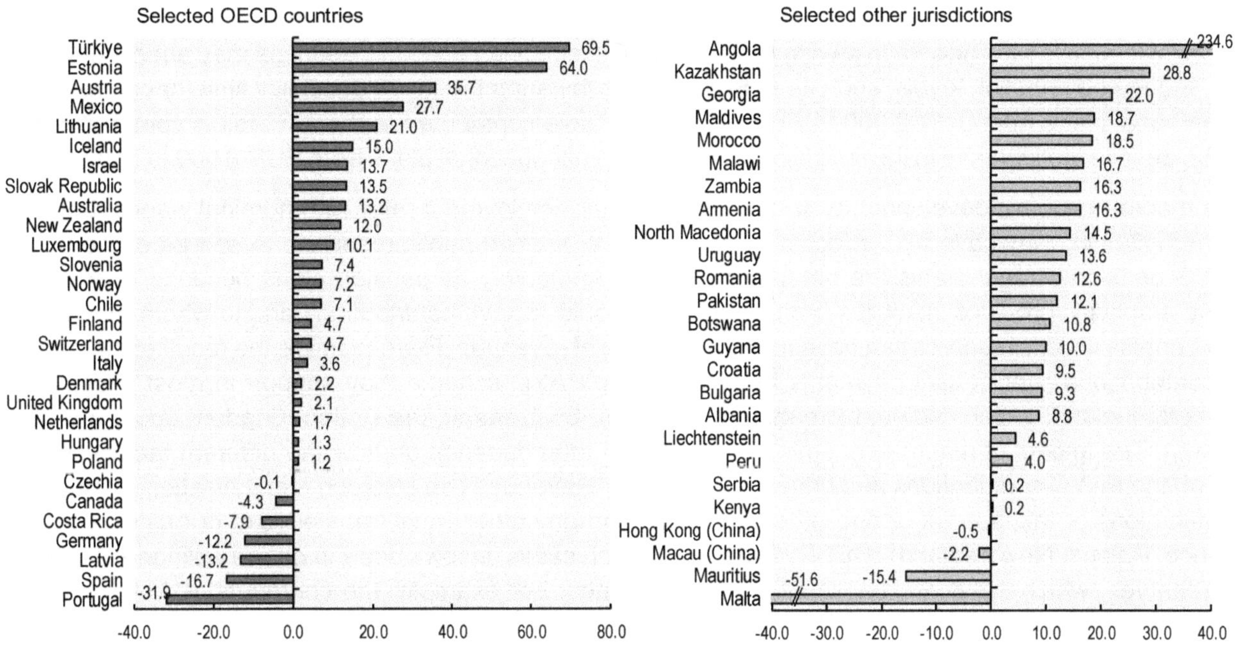

Note: For more details, please see the methodological notes in Annex C.
Source: OECD Global Pension Statistics.

StatLink https://stat.link/kdgsvi

The increase in nominal wages 2022 is also behind the increase in contributions. As inflation was rising in 2021 and most of 2022, nominal wages also rose with a lag, automatically increasing the amount of contributions paid when contributions are defined as a percentage of earnings. This effect was particularly visible on contributions paid in Türkiye where inflation was at 64% at end-2022 and nominal wages increased the most over the period 2019-22 in the OECD area (OECD, 2023[9]).

Some policy or supervisory measures may have reinforced the effect of wage growth on contribution levels in some countries. Some countries increased mandatory contributions rates (e.g. Australia from 10% to 10.5% in July 2022, the Slovak Republic from 5.25% to 5.5% in 2022), or simply returned to normal conditions after the suspension or reduction of mandatory contributions granted in the midst of the COVID-19 crisis (e.g. Estonia, Finland) (OECD, 2022[10]).[5] Norway expanded the earning base used to calculate mandatory contributions in 2022, requiring all employers to contribute 2% of the salary of their employees from the first krone up to 12G since 1 January 2022,[6] while there was often no contribution for salaries below 1G before.[7] Some supervisory authorities, especially in Africa, endeavoured to boost compliance with existing mandatory contribution rates to increase contributions. For example, the supervisor in Ghana took legal action against employers who did not comply with the 5% mandatory contribution rate. In Malawi, a part of the 17% increase in contributions in 2022 comes from a reduction in contribution arrears, although there was reportedly still a large amount of outstanding contributions unremitted to pension funds.

The rise in inflation and cost-of-living may have led some people to delay retirement, making them contribute for longer. According to different studies, the rise in cost of living led 41% of pre-retirees in the United Kingdom and 20% to 40% of older workers in the United States to delay retirement.[8] At the same time, it may have also led some people to stop or reduce voluntary contributions, due to the potential lower capacity to save for retirement and the higher priority they gave to other needs. The rise in interest rates following central banks' attempt to contain inflationary pressures may have also improved the financial position of defined benefit plans in some countries,[9] reducing the need for employers to make additional contributions to guarantee the promise, such as in Portugal (-32%).

Voluntary contributions to pension plans may also be sensitive to financial incentives. Many countries have financial incentives to encourage saving for retirement. Reducing financial incentives may affect behaviour and reduce contribution levels, such as in Spain where lowering the tax deductibility limit for contributions to personal plans from EUR 2 000 to EUR 1 500 may have contributed to the 17% fall in contributions in 2022, despite the increase in the limit for contributions to occupational plans from EUR 8 000 to EUR 8 500.

The macro-economic developments in 2022, with higher employment rates and nominal wages, but also higher inflation, may have also affected the revenues to finance public reserves. Reserves of the public PAYG pension arrangements are not financed in the same way as pension plans because they do not serve a specific group of members from whom they would receive contributions and to whom they would pay benefits. Public reserves can have multiple sources of revenues. Revenues are the result of the excess of contributions over benefit payments from the public PAYG scheme they support in most cases (e.g. Canada, Finland, Japan, Korea, Luxembourg, Sweden, Switzerland, the United Kingdom and the United States). The impact of macro-economic developments then depends on how the different factors played out on the PAYG contributions and benefit payments.[10] Revenues can also come privatisation, earmarked contributions or tax, special or one-off contribution, and any other fiscal transfer (e.g. in Australia, Chile, France, Poland, New Zealand) (OECD, 2021[11]). In such cases, inflows depend on the willingness to build up reserves, which the economic situation may influence. For example, the contributions to the reserve fund were suspended in 2020 and 2021 in Chile during the pandemic but resumed in 2022 following the economic recovery.

Notes

[1] Mandatory pension plans include mandatory occupational plans (where employers are required by law to set up a pension plan for their employees who then have to join the plan, e.g. Finland, Norway, Switzerland), quasi-mandatory occupational plans (where participation levels are high because plans are established through collective agreements at the industry or sector level, e.g. Denmark, the Netherlands, Sweden) and mandatory personal plans (where workers are required to join a pension plan, e.g. Chile, Colombia, Denmark, Mexico).

[2] This is particularly the case when the obligation to participate only applies to the youngest generations (e.g. those born in or after 1974 in Armenia, those under 40 in Georgia). In Bulgaria, the participation rate increased by eight percentage points as the number of participants in the second pension pillar (the numerator) increased while the working-age population (the denominator) shrank because of emigration (OECD, 2023[16]).

[3] Rise in opt-out rates prompts concern despite AE successes - Pensions Age Magazine

[4] See statistical annex (Annex B).

[5] In Estonia, the 4% employer contribution to the second pension pillar was suspended between 1 July 2020 and 31 August 2021. Contributions increased in 2022, despite the possibility given to members of the second pension pillar to stop contributing since the pension reform in 2021. In Finland, employer

contributions to earnings-related pension plans were lowered in 2020 due to the pandemic but this reduction is being fully compensated by an increase in contributions between 2022 and 2025.

[6] G is the National Base Amount.

[7] Norway extends pension scheme access - Lockton Global Benefits

[8] 2.5 million plan to delay retirement due to cost-of-living crisis | Legal & General (legalandgeneral.com) and US. 5 Ways Inflation is Changing Retirement Planning - Pension Policy International

[9] See following section 4.

[10] The study of the impacts of the macro-economic and financial environment on contributions and benefits paid from public PAYG schemes goes beyond the scope of this report. Please see OECD Pensions at a Glance 2023 for more information on this topic.

3 Investment losses led to a decline in the value of assets when the surplus of contributions over benefits was insufficient to offset them

Asset-backed pension systems incurred investment losses across the board, hampering asset growth. Assets earmarked for retirement declined in many OECD countries but were still on the rise in many non-OECD jurisdictions. Many non-OECD jurisdictions recorded an excess of contributions over benefits, which offset these investment losses.

This section shows the evolution of assets in 2022. It looks into the difference between the contributions pension plans received and the benefits they paid, and shows where the surplus offsets investment losses.

3.1. The value of assets earmarked for retirement dropped in 2022 in OECD countries

The value of assets earmarked for retirement fell in 2022 in the OECD area, contrasting with the long-term upward trend in the last decades (Figure 3.1). Assets in pension plans dropped by 14% in the OECD, from USD 59 trillion at end-2021 to USD 51 trillion at end-2022, the largest fall since the 2008 global financial crisis when assets dropped by 18%. Public reserves also shrank by 10% in 2022, more than during the 2008 global financial crisis when they fell by 4%.

Figure 3.1. Assets earmarked for retirement in the OECD, 2001-2022

In USD trillion

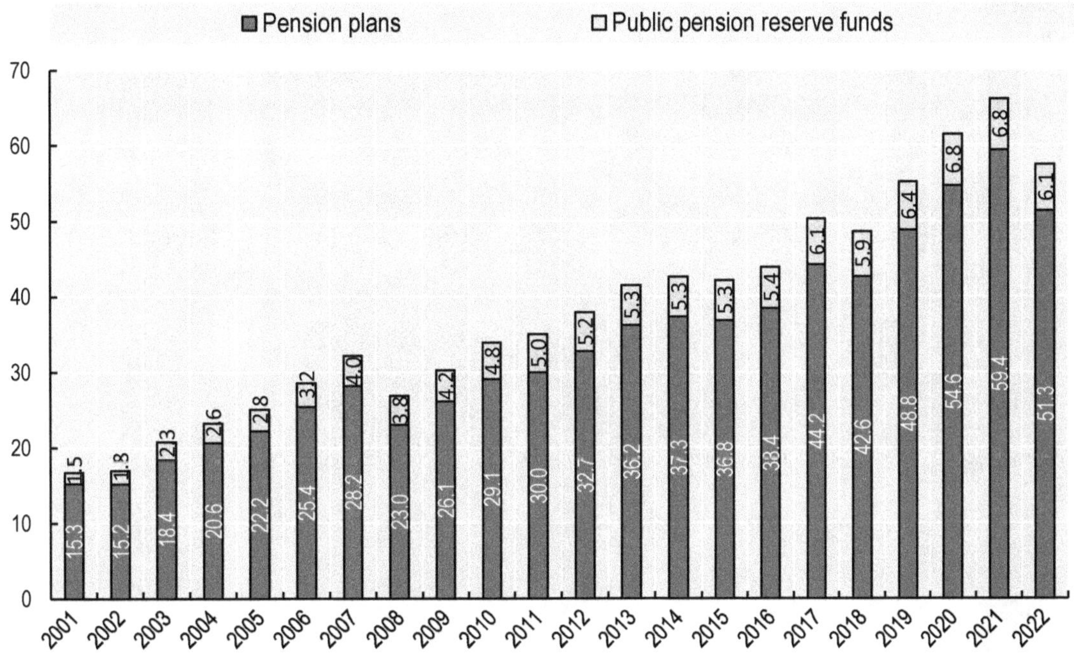

Note: For more details, please see the methodological notes in Annex C.
Source: OECD Global Pension Statistics and other sources.

StatLink https://stat.link/o1xlei

This overall decline in total assets in 2022 was driven by the losses that the largest pension markets experienced. The United States is the country with the largest amount of assets in pension plans at end-2022 (USD 35 trillion), followed by Canada, the United Kingdom, Australia, the Netherlands, Switzerland and Japan where assets amounted to between USD 1 and 4 trillion (Figure 3.2). When expressed in national currency, the amount of assets in all these large markets declined, between 6% (Canada) and 24% (United Kingdom) (Figure 3.3). Similarly, the largest public reserves dropped in 2022, by 1% for the United States Old-Age and Survivors Insurance (OASI) Trust Fund, by 5% for Japan's Government Pension Investment Fund (GPIF), and by 6% for Korea's reserves in the Government Employees Pension Fund (GEPF) and the National Pension Fund (NPF).[1] These declines become even larger when expressed in current US dollars (e.g. -31.9% for the United Kingdom, -17.9% for Japan's GPIF and -12% for Korea's reserves in GEPF and NPF) as the US dollar appreciated against some of the major currencies in 2022.

Figure 3.2. Assets earmarked for retirement around the world at end-2022

In USD trillion

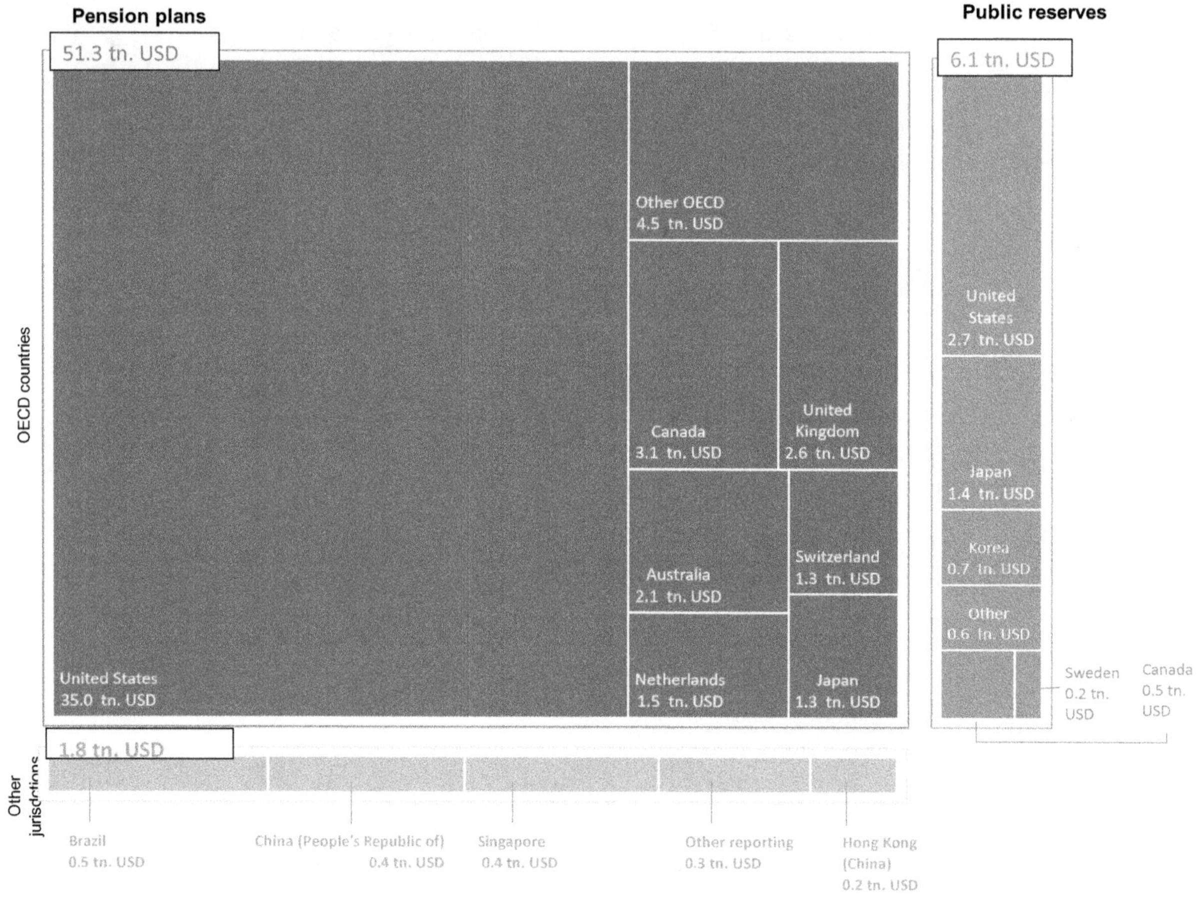

Note: For more details, please see the methodological notes in Annex C.
Source: OECD Global Pension Statistics and other sources.

https://stat.link/o9vxmy

Figure 3.3. Nominal growth rate of assets earmarked for retirement, by country, 2022

In per cent

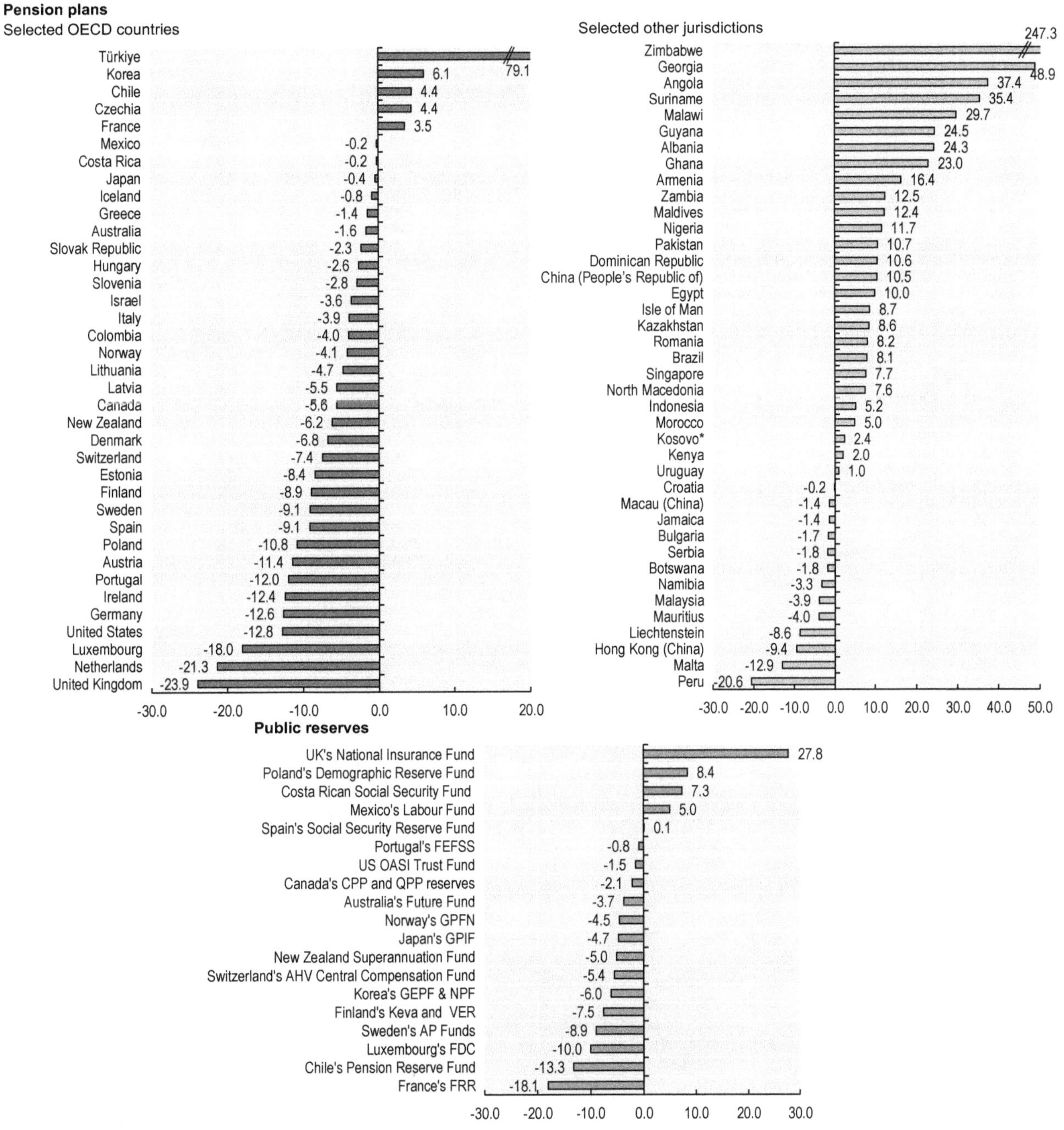

Note: For more details, please see the methodological notes in Annex C.
Source: OECD Global Pension Statistics and other sources.

StatLink https://stat.link/7452ao

Pension assets represented a smaller share of the domestic economy in most reporting jurisdictions at end-2022 than a year before (Figure 3.4). While nominal GDP rose in 2022, assets earmarked for retirement declined in most OECD countries, or increased at a slower pace than GDP in many non-OECD jurisdictions. There was no OECD country where assets in pension plans exceeded twice the GDP at end-

2022, unlike at end-2021 in Denmark (229%), Iceland (218%) and the Netherlands (211%). Denmark remained the country with the largest amount of assets in pension plans at end-2022, worth 192% of GDP. Korea also remained the OECD country with the largest amount of public reserves relative to the size of its economy at end-2022 (42% of GDP).

Figure 3.4. Assets earmarked for retirement, by country, at end-2021 and end-2022

As a percentage of GDP

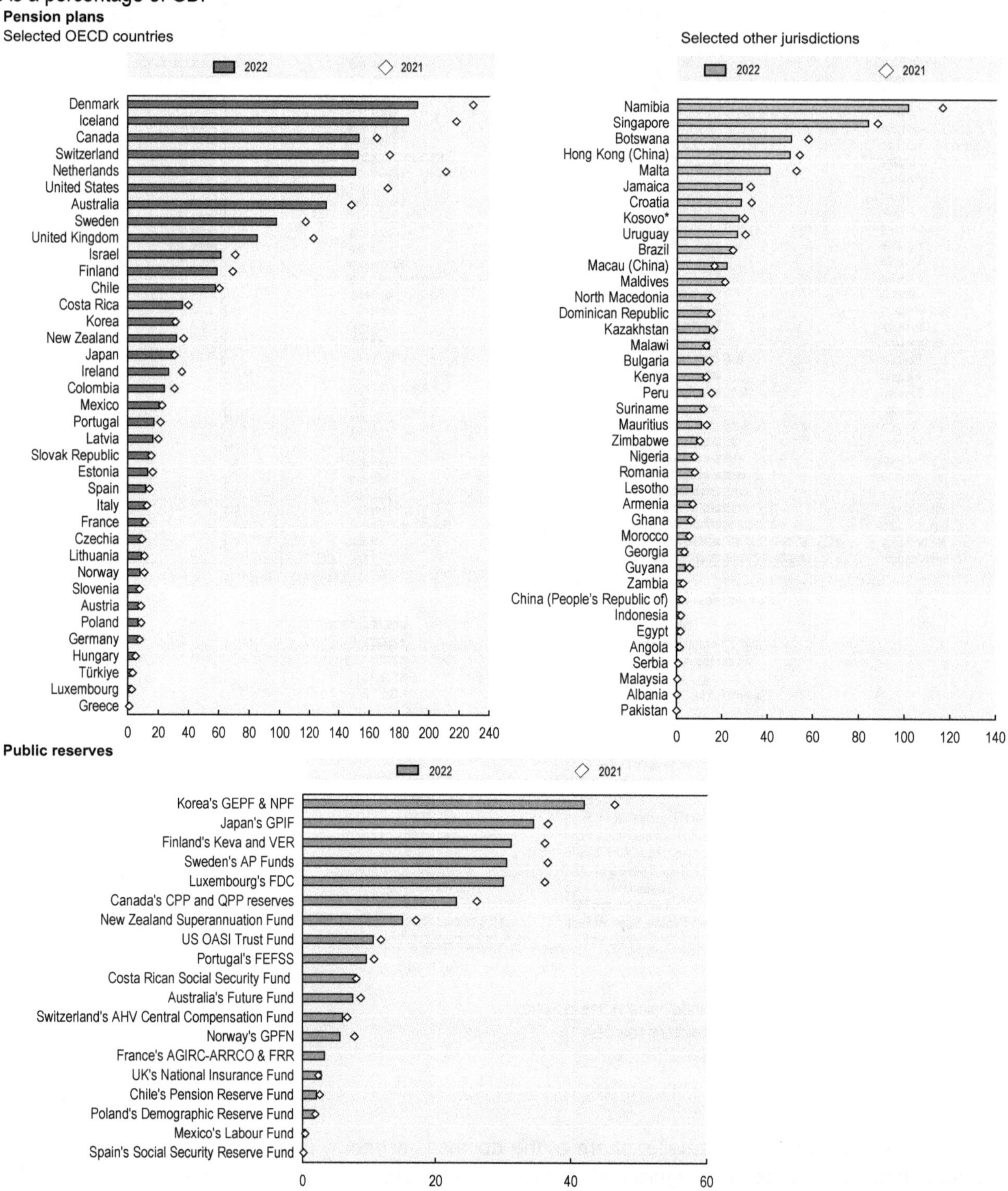

Source: OECD Global Pension Statistics and other sources.

StatLink https://stat.link/gi6lth

3.2. Contributions were higher than benefits paid in many jurisdictions

Many jurisdictions experienced a surplus of contributions over benefits (Figure 3.5). Pension systems that are mainly in the accumulation phase and where pension benefit payments have not or just started may experience surpluses of contributions over benefits. By contrast, countries with more mature pension systems in which a larger share of the population receives pension benefits may have a negative balance between contributions and benefits (e.g. Canada, United Kingdom).

Figure 3.5. Contributions and pension benefits flows from pension plans, 2022

As a percentage of GDP

Selected OECD countries

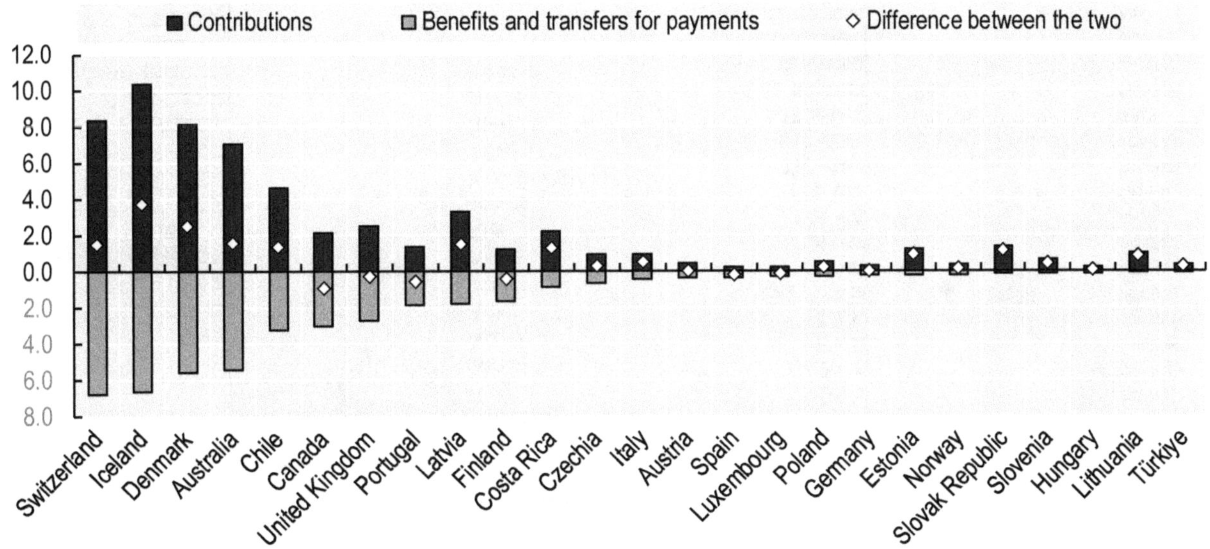

Selected other jurisdictions

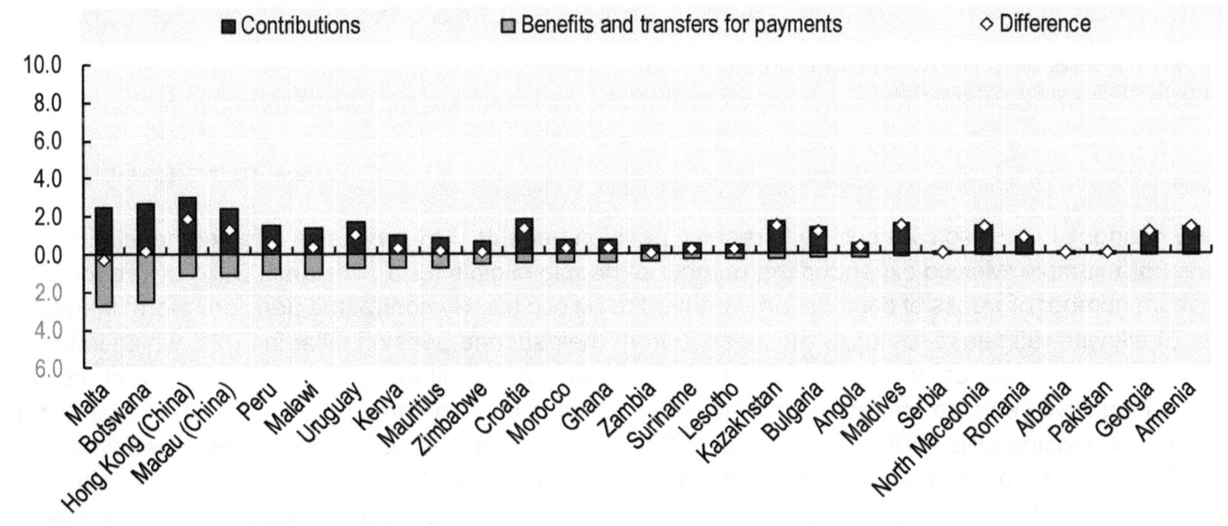

Note: For more details, please see the methodological notes in Annex C.
Source: OECD Global Pension Statistics.

StatLink https://stat.link/63g087

Benefit payments increased in most jurisdictions in 2022 (Figure 3.6) although they did not reach the level of contributions.[2] Inflation partially accounted for this increase. This is the case in countries where there is at least partial indexation of pensions to inflation (e.g. Netherlands, United Kingdom, South Africa). Inflation may have also increased the level of drawdown payments when retirees could choose the amount to withdraw (e.g. Hungary). Benefit payments have been increasing rapidly in jurisdictions where the pay-out phase is starting and the system is maturing (e.g. Armenia, Serbia, North Macedonia).

Figure 3.6. Nominal growth rate of pension benefit flows from pension plans, 2022

In per cent

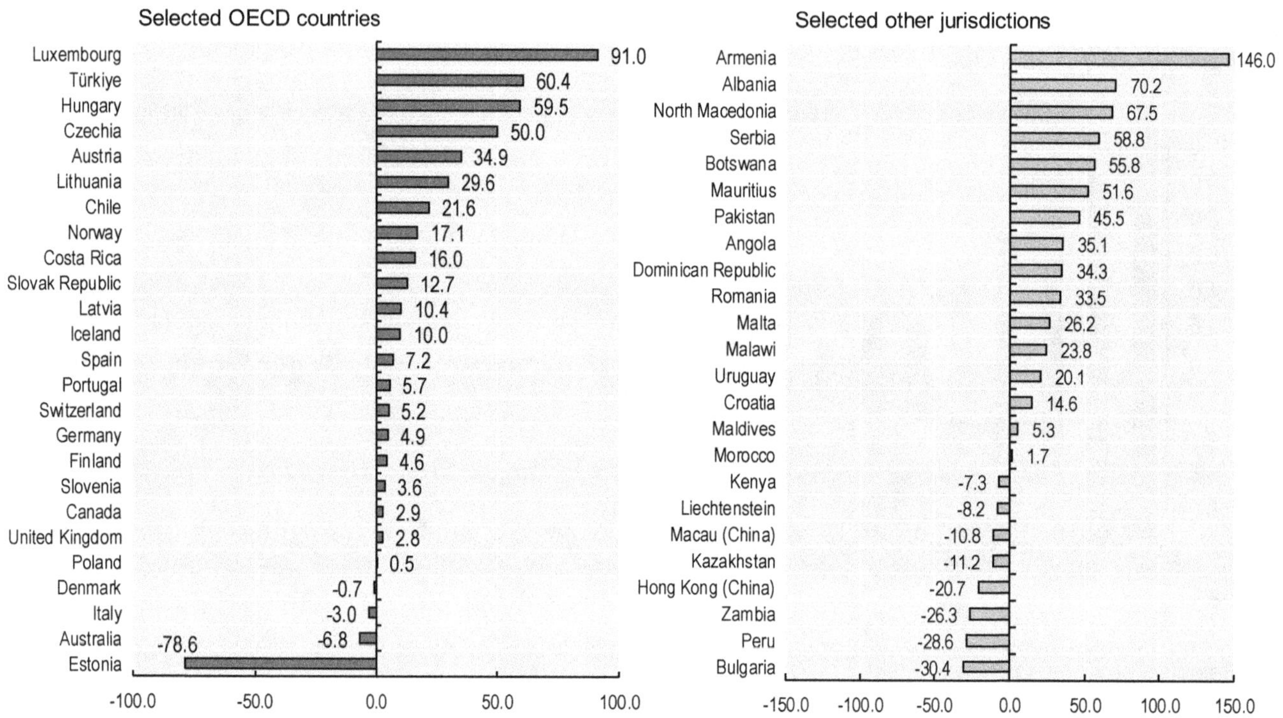

Note: For more details, please see the methodological notes in Annex C.
Source: OECD Global Pension Statistics.

StatLink https://stat.link/9idoqt

Policy changes to the eligibility criteria to receive pension benefits may have also affected pension benefit flows. For example, Mexico expanded the number of people eligible for a pension in 2021 by reducing the minimum number of weeks of contributions required to be eligible. By contrast, a pension reform in Estonia in 2020 allowed retirees to withdraw the balance from their second pension pillar in 2021, which led to an exceptional rise in one-off payments in 2021, with effects wearing off in 2022. In Bulgaria, members who had less than five years before retirement and who had not done so before could transfer their assets from the second pension pillar to the first pillar in 2021 to receive only a public pension. Retirees who were already receiving a pension from the first pillar in Bulgaria could also benefit from this option and transfer their assets from the second pillar. This option in 2021 resulted in exceptional transfers to the first pillar in 2021, accounting for the 30% drop in the benefit flows from the asset-backed pension system in 2022.

3.3. The surplus of contributions over benefits was insufficient to offset investment losses in most jurisdictions

The surplus of contributions was not sufficient to offset investment losses in any OECD country in 2022. Table 3.1 shows in blue the negative nominal rates of return, the deficit between contributions and pension payments and the resulting negative nominal growth rate of assets. The decline of assets in the OECD area resulted from investment losses incurred in 2022. The largest loss of pension plan assets happened in the Netherlands and the United Kingdom, where pension plans had the lowest nominal returns among all reporting jurisdictions (-21.1% and -18.5% respectively).

Table 3.1. Asset growth and its main underlying drivers for pension plans in selected OECD and non-OECD jurisdictions, in 2022

Selected OECD countries	Nominal Investment Rates of Return (%)	Surplus contributions over benefits (as % GDP)	Nominal growth rate of assets (%)
Netherlands	-21.1	..	-21.3
United Kingdom	-18.5	-0.2	-23.9
Poland	-16.1	0.2	-10.8
Latvia	-15.0	1.5	-5.5
Lithuania	-14.7	0.9	-4.7
Luxembourg	-14.6	-0.1	-18.0
Denmark	-14.2	2.6	-6.8
Ireland	-13.6	..	-12.4
United States	-12.8	..	-12.8
Portugal	-10.5	-0.5	-12.0
Austria	-10.2	0.0	-11.4
Switzerland	-9.5	1.5	-7.4
Estonia	-9.2	1.0	-8.4
Spain	-9.0	-0.2	-9.1
Greece	-8.8	..	-1.4
Slovak Republic	-8.7	1.2	-2.3
Costa Rica	-7.7	1.3	-0.2
Italy	-7.3	0.5	-3.9
Slovenia	-7.3	0.4	-2.8
Hungary	-7.1	0.1	-2.6
Norway	-5.7	0.2	-4.1
Finland	-5.1	-0.4	-8.9
Colombia	-4.2	..	-4.0
Mexico	-4.1	..	-0.2
Israel	-3.8	..	-3.6
Iceland	-3.3	3.7	-0.8
Canada	-3.1	-0.9	-5.6
Australia	-1.9	1.6	-1.6
Germany	-1.2	0.0	-12.6
Czechia	0.4	0.3	4.4
Chile	3.0	1.4	4.4
Türkiye	49.6	0.3	79.1

Selected other jurisdictions	Nominal Investment Rates of Return (%)	Surplus contributions over benefits (as % GDP)	Nominal growth rate of assets (%)
Hong Kong (China)	-15.4	1.8	-9.4
Liechtenstein	-11.9	..	-8.6
Bulgaria	-10.3	1.1	-1.7
Peru	-8.2	0.5	-20.6
Macau (China)	-8.2	1.3	-1.4
Malta	-8.1	-0.3	-12.9
Armenia	-7.9	1.4	16.4
Kosovo*	-5.4	..	2.4
Croatia	-5.2	1.3	-0.2
Romania	-3.1	0.8	8.2
North Macedonia	-2.4	1.4	7.6
Serbia	-1.2	0.0	-1.8
Uruguay	-0.8	1.0	1.0
Namibia	-0.8	..	-3.3
Morocco	1.5	0.3	5.0
Kenya	2.6	0.3	2.0
Guyana	3.0	..	24.5
Albania	3.8	0.1	24.3
Maldives	4.3	1.4	12.4
Pakistan	5.0	0.0	10.7
Dominican Republic	5.3	..	10.6
Indonesia	5.5	..	5.2
Botswana	5.5	0.2	-1.8
Kazakhstan	6.3	1.4	8.6
Georgia	7.4	1.1	48.9
Nigeria	8.2	..	11.7
Angola	9.0	0.4	37.4
Egypt	11.3	..	10.0
Zambia	12.7	0.0	12.5
Ghana	17.7	0.3	23.0
Malawi	19.6	0.4	29.7
Suriname	19.7	0.2	35.4
Zimbabwe	54.5	0.1	247.3

Note: Cells in blue show negative values.
Source: OECD Global Pension Statistics.

StatLink https://stat.link/ktyxhf

By contrast, many non-OECD jurisdictions managed to record a positive nominal growth rate of assets in 2022, even in some of them that incurred nominal investment losses (e.g. Armenia, North Macedonia, Romania). The surplus of contributions over benefits offset investment losses in these cases. However, this surplus was insufficient even in non-OECD jurisdictions where the investment losses were the largest.

Other outflows or leakages from pension plans can happen before retirement and slow asset growth. In Kenya, when people change jobs, they can and tend to access their savings, which has been a hindrance in asset growth for years according to the supervisor. A number of countries allow members to access their assets before retirement for different motives (e.g. home purchase, financial hardship, illness) (OECD, 2019[12]). Some countries have facilitated access to retirement savings during COVID-19. For example, Peru granted access to assets in individual accounts six times between 2020 and 2022. Over six million members had seized this opportunity by end-2022, accounting for the 21% decline in assets in 2022. Since its 2021 pension reform, Estonia has been giving the possibility for members up to 5 years before the retirement age to withdraw all their savings from the second pension pillar (with no other condition), and around 214 000 people applied to do so by end-2022. In the context of rising inflation, some members may have also seized the opportunity to withdraw some of their retirement savings to cope with rising prices, such as in the United States: 32% of members tapped into their retirement account (IRA or 401(k) plan) to cope with inflation according to a US News & World Report survey. [3]

Outflows from public pension reserve funds are different from those of pension plans. For public reserves financed through the excess of contributions over benefits of public PAYG schemes, outflows would be triggered when current benefits exceed current contributions, as in Finland and Sweden. For the others financed through budget transfers, the law usually stipulates the circumstances or dates when assets can be used (e.g. Australia, New Zealand).

Public reserves in Spain and Canada (for the Quebec Pension Plan) were the only ones to grow despite investment losses in 2022 (Figure 3.7). Positive cashflows offset investment losses in these two cases. By contrast, assets in the United States OASI Trust Fund declined despite a positive interest rate in 2022 as the total expenditure of the fund exceeded its revenues.[4]

Figure 3.7. Nominal investment rates of return (IRRs) and asset growth of selected public pension reserve funds in the OECD area, in 2022

In per cent

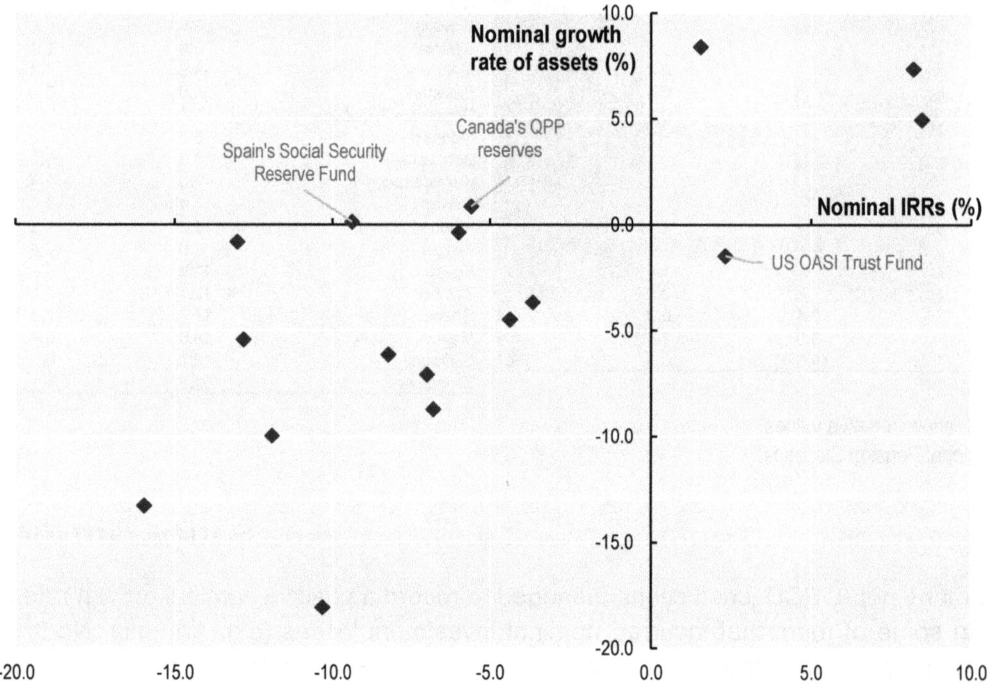

Source: OECD Global Pension Statistics and other sources.

StatLink https://stat.link/sqcdh5

Notes

[1] Reserves of the US OASI Trust Fund, Japan's GPIF and Korea's funds amounted to USD 2.7 trillion, USD 1.4 trillion and USD 0.7 trillion respectively at end-2022.

[2] There are different types of pay-out choices depending on the jurisdictions (e.g. one-off lump sum, pension, regular withdrawals, or a combination). Individuals may receive their pension benefits from the entity that managed the assets during the accumulation phase, or from another entity (e.g. an insurance company, the social security institute). In the latter, the assets are transferred to the other entity at the time of retirement.

[3] Retirement Inflation Survey | U.S. News (usnews.com)

[4] OASI Trust Fund, a Social Security fund (ssa.gov)

4 Increase in interest rates improved the sustainability of some defined benefit pension plans

Members of traditional defined benefit plans are generally guaranteed to receive a benefit based on the length of employment, an accrual rate and their final or average salary. A decline in the value of pension assets is not expected to have a direct impact on the benefits that people will receive in defined benefit (DB) pension plans. The sponsor of the plan (generally the employer) is responsible for covering any gap or shortfall between the amount of assets in the plan and the liabilities arising from the promise, generally through additional contributions.

Changes in inflation, interest rates and labour market developments can affect the present value of the benefit promise that some sponsors offer in the pension plan they set up for their employees. The evolution of employment rates and wages can affect entitlements and future benefit payments when the benefit formula is based on the length of employment and wages. Also, these future payments are liabilities for DB plans and need to be expressed in today's terms to calculate the amount to be held as technical reserves to cover these promises. The lower the discount rate is to express these future payments in today's terms, the higher the estimation of liabilities is. This discount rate can be tied to the evolution of interest rates.

Liabilities of DB plans have been rising over the last two decades as interest rates fell. Figure 4.1 shows the increase in liabilities and their volatility. They are volatile when they are sensitive to changes in the parameters and assumptions underlying their calculations. However, in a context of low and falling interest rates for many years, the liabilities tended to rise for DB plans in all reporting jurisdictions.

Figure 4.1. Evolution of the liabilities of defined benefit plans in selected jurisdictions, 2001-2022

Base: 2021 = 100

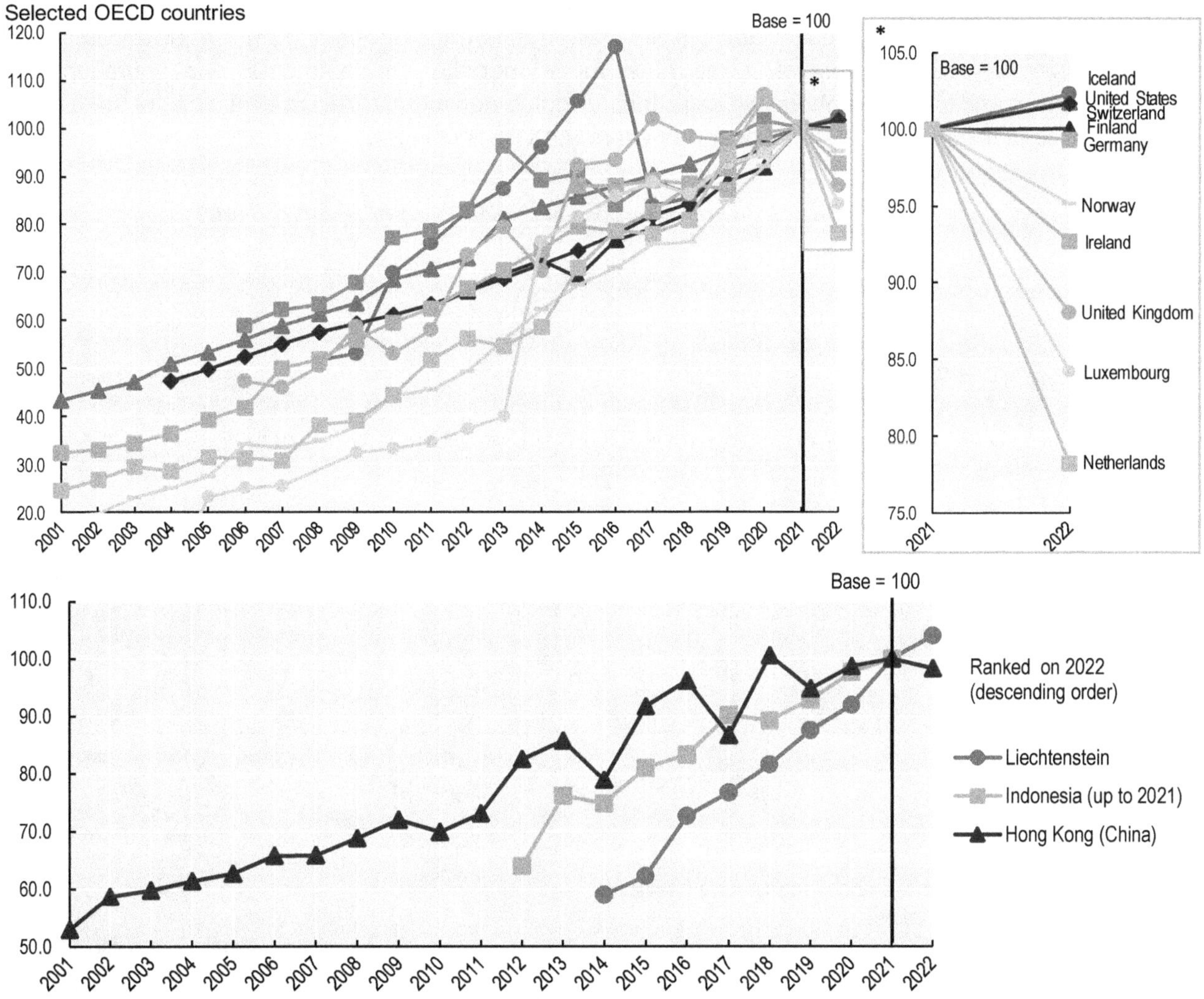

Note: For more details, please see the methodological notes in Annex C.
Source: OECD Global Pension Statistics.

StatLink https://stat.link/2zbf0t

Liabilities dropped in most reporting jurisdictions in 2022 as interest rates rose. Some of the sharpest drops occurred in the United Kingdom (12%) and the Netherlands (22%) where future obligations of the plan are expressed in today's terms based on market-based rates. The increase in interest rates lowered the estimated value of future obligations.

However, in jurisdictions where the calculation of liabilities is with a fixed interest rate, the change in interest rates did not affect the value of liabilities (e.g. Finland (3%) and Iceland (3.5%)). *Pensionskassen* in Germany also have to use a fixed discount rate under the local Generally Accepted Accounting Principles (GAAP) to calculate liabilities. Therefore, in these countries, the change in interest rates did not affect the valuation of liabilities, which remained broadly at the same level in 2022 compared to 2021 (such as in Finland and Germany) or even increased (such as in Iceland, by 2%). In Switzerland, although this is not mandated, some pension funds maintained their technical interest rate as it was to value the liabilities for plans in benefit primacy (i.e. where benefits are based on tenure and last salary), which may partly explain the overall increase in liabilities in 2022.

Therefore, the financial sustainability of DB plans improved in some jurisdictions despite the fall in assets, as liabilities fell as well. Liabilities of DB plans fell more than assets in Luxembourg, the Netherlands, Norway and the United Kingdom (Figure 4.2). By contrast, the funding ratio of DB plans worsened in jurisdictions where the liabilities remained the same or slightly increased (e.g. Germany, Iceland, Finland, Switzerland and the United States). Liabilities are valued differently depending on the jurisdictions and methodological choices regarding discount rates, future mortality improvements, and approach with respect to current and future members, which probably contributed to the different evolutions of the funding ratios across jurisdictions in 2022 as in previous years (OECD, 2023[4]).

Figure 4.2. Funding ratio of defined benefit plans in selected jurisdictions, 2021-2022

In per cent

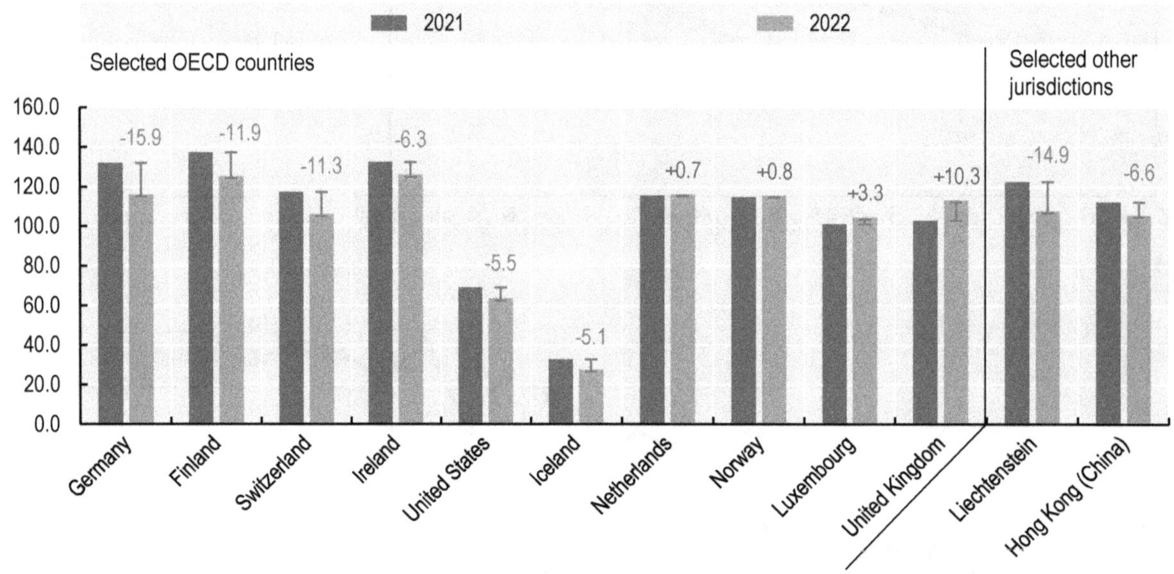

Note: For more details, please see the methodological notes in Annex C.
Source: OECD Global Pension Statistics.

StatLink https://stat.link/sf5byv

Assets in DB plans in most reporting jurisdictions would have been sufficient at end-2022 to cover the liabilities arising from the benefit promise. The funding ratio exceeded 100% at end-2022 in all reporting jurisdictions except Iceland (28%) and the United States (64%). However, the aggregated funding ratios at end-2022 may hide disparities in the solvency of the many DB plans that exist within each country.

Some DB plans with improved funding ratios have been looking into the possibility to lock-in the gains by going into buy-out and transferring their assets and liabilities to insurance companies. The number of buy-outs has been rising in the United Kingdom and the United States for instance.[1] There had been concerns over the potential challenges this rise in pension risk transfer could entail (e.g. on the supply side through supply-chain bottlenecks) but this does not seem to have been a problem in practice according to some of the insurers operating in this market.[2]

Notes

[1] Lane Clark & Peacock LLP (lcp.com) (for the United Kingdom); LIMRA (for the United States)

[2] No capacity issues in the buyout market, WPC told - Pensions Age Magazine

5 The recent macro-economic developments indirectly impacted fees levied in 2022

Pension providers levied more fees in 2022 than in 2021 in most reporting jurisdictions. Table 5.1 shows that the amount of fees collected increased the most in several non-OECD jurisdictions (Albania, Liechtenstein, the Maldives and North Macedonia). By contrast, fees declined in some countries, with the largest drop recorded in the Slovak Republic (-55%).

Table 5.1. Evolution of the amount of fees levied in 2022 relative to 2021

In per cent

Country	ISO code	Change in total fees
Slovak Republic	SVK	-54.5
Romania	ROU	-45.0
Mexico	MEX	-26.4
Colombia	COL	-24.2
Kazakhstan	KAZ	-20.8
Hungary	HUN	-7.3
Poland	POL	-5.9
Slovenia	SVN	0.3
Czechia	CZE	1.1
Chile	CHL	1.5
Bulgaria	BGR	2.1
Croatia	HRV	2.1
Pakistan	PAK	2.9
Peru	PER	3.3
Costa Rica	CRI	7.4
Lithuania	LTU	8.5
Albania	ALB	11.8
North Macedonia	MKD	13.2
Maldives	MDV	14.9
Liechtenstein	LIE	24.4

Source: OECD Global Pension Statistics.

StatLink https://stat.link/aprf84

Higher inflation, higher interest rates and improvements in labour markets also affected the fees charged to members of DC plans in 2022. Fees can be charged on contributions or on salaries directly as in some Latin American countries (e.g. Chile, Colombia), on assets (e.g. Estonia, Spain), on performance, or a combination (e.g. Czechia, Bulgaria).[1] Fees on assets are the most widespread way pension providers charge members for services (OECD, 2023[4]). On top of regular fees, members in some jurisdictions can be charged fees when they join, switch or leave a pension provider (e.g. Albania, Czechia, Hungary).

The aggregated amount of fees charged on contributions increased in most jurisdictions where this type of fee exists (Figure 5.1). The rising levels of contributions in 2022 generally led to larger amounts of fees levied on members (top left panel of Figure 5.1). Romania is an exception, as fees on contributions dropped despite the overall increase in contributions.[2]

Figure 5.1. Evolution of fees charged to members relative to contributions, assets and the investment performance of the plans, 2022

In per cent

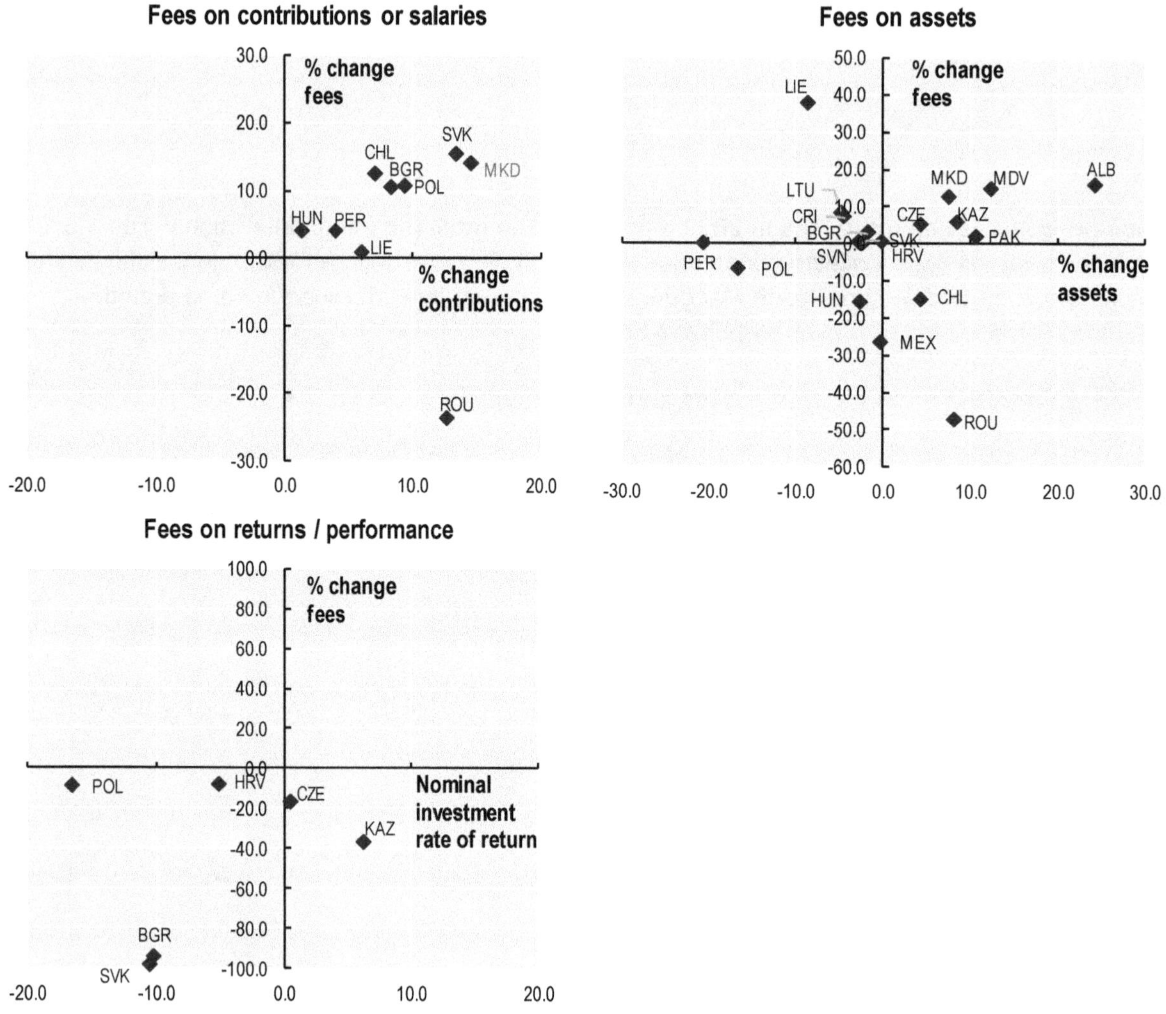

Note: Jurisdictions are labelled with their ISO codes in the charts.
Source: OECD Global Pension Statistics.

StatLink https://stat.link/2b5r69

Fees charged on assets also tended to vary with assets. There are some exceptions (top right panel of Figure 5.1). For example, fees on assets decreased in Chile and Romania despite the rise in pension assets. In Chile, this is because the investment expenses that pension funds incurred declined in 2022. In Romania, the fee cap on assets increases with the extent to which the nominal investment rate of return exceeds the inflation rate. Given that Romanian pension funds achieved negative real returns overall in 2022 (Figure 1.2), the fee cap was at its lowest possible level (0.02% monthly). Conversely, fees levied on assets increased in 2022 while the amount of pension assets declined in 2022 in some countries due to the way fees are calculated. For example, in Costa Rica and Lithuania, pension providers charge fees on the amount of assets daily and the average amount of assets was higher in 2022 than in 2021.

Pension providers charging fees on investment performance all collected lower amounts of fees in 2022 than in 2021 (bottom left panel of Figure 5.1). The largest drop occurred in in the Slovak Republic that uses of a high-water mark. The high-water mark mechanism in the Slovak Republic only triggers a fee collection when the unit value of the portfolio exceeds the last highest value over the last three years (for the second pillar) or since the beginning of 2010 (for the third pillar). Given the low investment performance in 2022, almost no performance fee was collected.

Overall, fees were among the highest as a percentage of assets in Albania, Türkiye and Uruguay (Table 5.2) where fees are charged on contributions or assets. However, higher levels of fees, expressed as a percentage of assets, do not necessarily imply that a system is more expensive overall for plan members than another one. Fee structures vary across jurisdictions, and fees charged on contributions (but expressed as a percentage of assets) may seem higher than in countries charging on assets only, especially in the early years of the system where contributions (and therefore fees on contributions) represent a larger share of assets under management (OECD, 2022[8]).

Table 5.2. Annual fees charged to members of defined contribution plans by type of fees, 2022

As a percentage of total assets in the plans

	Fees on salaries	Fees on contributions	Fees on assets	Fees on returns / performance	Other fees
Selected OECD countries					
Australia (1)			0.4		
Chile	0.6	x	0.3	x	x
Colombia (2)	0.3	x	x	x	0.2
Costa Rica (3)	x	x	0.4	x	x
Czechia	x	x	0.8	0.1	0.0
Estonia	x	x	0.6	0.0	0.0
Hungary (4)	x	0.4	0.4	..	..
Lithuania	x	..	0.5	..	0.0
Mexico (5)	x	x	0.5	x	x
Poland (6)	x	0.0	0.5	0.0	x
Slovak Republic	x	0.1	0.4	0.0	0.0
Slovenia	x	..	0.8	x	..
Spain (5)	x	x	1.1	..	x
Türkiye	x	0.1	1.4	x	0.4
Selected other jurisdictions					
Albania	x	x	1.8	x	0.2
Bulgaria	x	0.4	0.7	0.0	0.0
Croatia	x	0.0	0.3	0.0	0.0
Kazakhstan	x	x	0.1	0.1	x
Liechtenstein	x	0.2	0.4	x	0.0
Maldives	x	x	0.4	x	x
North Macedonia	x	0.2	0.4	x	..
Pakistan	x	x	1.2	x	0.0
Peru	0.9	x	0.2	x	x
Romania	x	0.0	0.3	x	0.0
Uruguay	x	6.5	x	x	x

Note: "x" means that the type of fee does not exist or is not allowed in the country. For more details, please see the methodological notes in Annex C.
Source: OECD Global Pension Statistics.

StatLink https://stat.link/03lmqk

Many jurisdictions have been lowering fee caps to reduce the fees charged to members. This includes Costa Rica, Croatia, the Maldives, and Romania. Only a few countries have provided or considered to provide greater flexibility to the cap, such as the United Kingdom that exempted performance fees from the 0.75% fee cap in 2023 to bolster investments in illiquid assets such as infrastructure.[3]

Some countries have also introduced structural solutions to reduce the fees charged by the industry or improve value for money. Chile, New Zealand and Peru have auction mechanisms for the selection of default funds, which aim at driving fees down. Pension providers in Chile and Peru bid on fees charged to members. The winning pension provider receives all new eligible entrants for a period of two years. In New Zealand, default providers are selected for a period of seven years based on a range of selection criteria that include fees. In Australia, the pension supervisor publishes heatmaps highlighting underperformance and high fees of superannuation product offerings, so as to urge trustees to reduce fees and review investment performance. In Hong Kong (China), the Mandatory Provident Fund Schemes Authority (i.e. the pension supervisor) is developing a common and integrated electronic platform (the eMPF Platform), which seeks to standardise, streamline and automate the administration processes of MPF schemes, thereby enhancing operational efficiency and reducing the overall costs of the MPF System, which should drive down the fees that members pay.[4]

Notes

[1] Pension funds in Czechia can charge fees on assets and profits. Supplementary voluntary pension funds in Bulgaria can charge fees on contributions and returns.

[2] Legal changes removed the possibility for pension fund management companies to charge fees on contributions to cover their administration costs towards the end of 2022. This contributed to the decline in fees that pension fund management companies charged on contributions in 2022.

[3] Focus on value from DC pension investments set to increase after regulation changes | The Pensions Regulator

[4] eMPF Platform Overview - MPFA

References

Alderman, A., K. Camp and E. Mandiak (2023), "How currency appreciation can impact prices: the rise of the U.S. dollar", *Beyond the Numbers: Prices & Spending*, Vol. 12/6, https://www.bls.gov/opub/btn/volume-12/how-currency-appreciation-can-impact-prices-the-rise-of-the-us-dollar.htm. [2]

FIAP (2018), *Investment Portfolios of the Latin American Pension Funds*. [15]

ILO (2020), *Global Employment Policy Review 2020: Employment policies for inclusive structural*, International Labour Office, https://www.ilo.org/wcmsp5/groups/public/---ed_emp/---ifp_skills/documents/publication/wcms_734489.pdf. [7]

Mesa-Lago, C. (2020), *Evaluation of Four Decades of Pension Privatization in Latin America, 1980-2020: Promises and Reality*. [14]

OECD (2023), *Annual Survey of Investment Regulation of Pension Providers 2023*, https://www.oecd.org/pensions/annualsurveyofinvestmentregulationofpensionfunds.htm. [1]

OECD (2023), *Nominal average wage growth in OECD countries, 2010-2022: Average annual growth in wages (percentage), 2010-19 and 2019-22*, OECD Publishing, https://doi.org/10.1787/6ac09bac-en. [9]

OECD (2023), *OECD Economic Surveys: Bulgaria 2023*, OECD Publishing, https://doi.org/10.1787/5ca812a4-en. [16]

OECD (2023), *OECD inflation slows further to 9.4% in December 2022*, https://www.oecd.org/sdd/prices-ppp/consumer-prices-oecd-02-2023.pdf. [3]

OECD (2023), *Pension Markets in Focus 2022*, https://www.oecd.org/finance/pensionmarketsinfocus.htm. [4]

OECD (2022), *Annual survey on financial incentives for retirement savings*, https://www.oecd.org/daf/fin/private-pensions/financial-incentives-retirement-savings-country-profiles-2022.pdf. [6]

OECD (2022), *OECD Pensions Outlook 2022*, OECD Publishing, https://doi.org/10.1787/20c7f443-en. [8]

OECD (2022), *Strengthening Asset-backed Pension Systems in a Post-COVID World*, OECD Publishing, https://doi.org/10.1787/288cb3cf-en. [10]

OECD (2021), *Pension Markets in Focus 2021*, https://www.oecd.org/finance/pensionmarketsinfocus.htm. [11]

OECD (2019), *Pensions at a Glance 2019: OECD and G20 Indicators*, OECD Publishing, https://doi.org/10.1787/b6d3dcfc-en. [12]

Office for National Statistics (2023), *Funded occupational pension schemes in the UK: October to December 2022*, https://www.ons.gov.uk/economy/investmentspensionsandtrusts/bulletins/fundedoccupationalpensionschemesintheuk/octobertodecember2022. [17]

Oh, S. and D. Stańko (2023), *Liquidity risks for pension funds related to margin calls: Survey results*, https://www.iopsweb.org/WP-41-Liquidity-risks-for-pension-funds-related-to-margin-calls.pdf. [5]

Stewart, F. and J. Yermo (2008), “Pension Fund Governance: Challenges and Potential Solutions”, *OECD Working Papers on Insurance and Private Pensions*, No. 18, OECD Publishing, Paris, https://doi.org/10.1787/241402256531. [13]

Annex A. Features of asset-backed pension systems

Asset-backed pension systems include various types of arrangements around the world. These arrangements finance the benefits of retirees in different ways, through specific vehicles administered by different entities (Figure A A.1). The way individuals get access to these arrangements and the type of benefits offered also vary across jurisdictions.

Figure A A.1. Features of asset-backed pension arrangements and evolution of the scope of Pension Markets in Focus

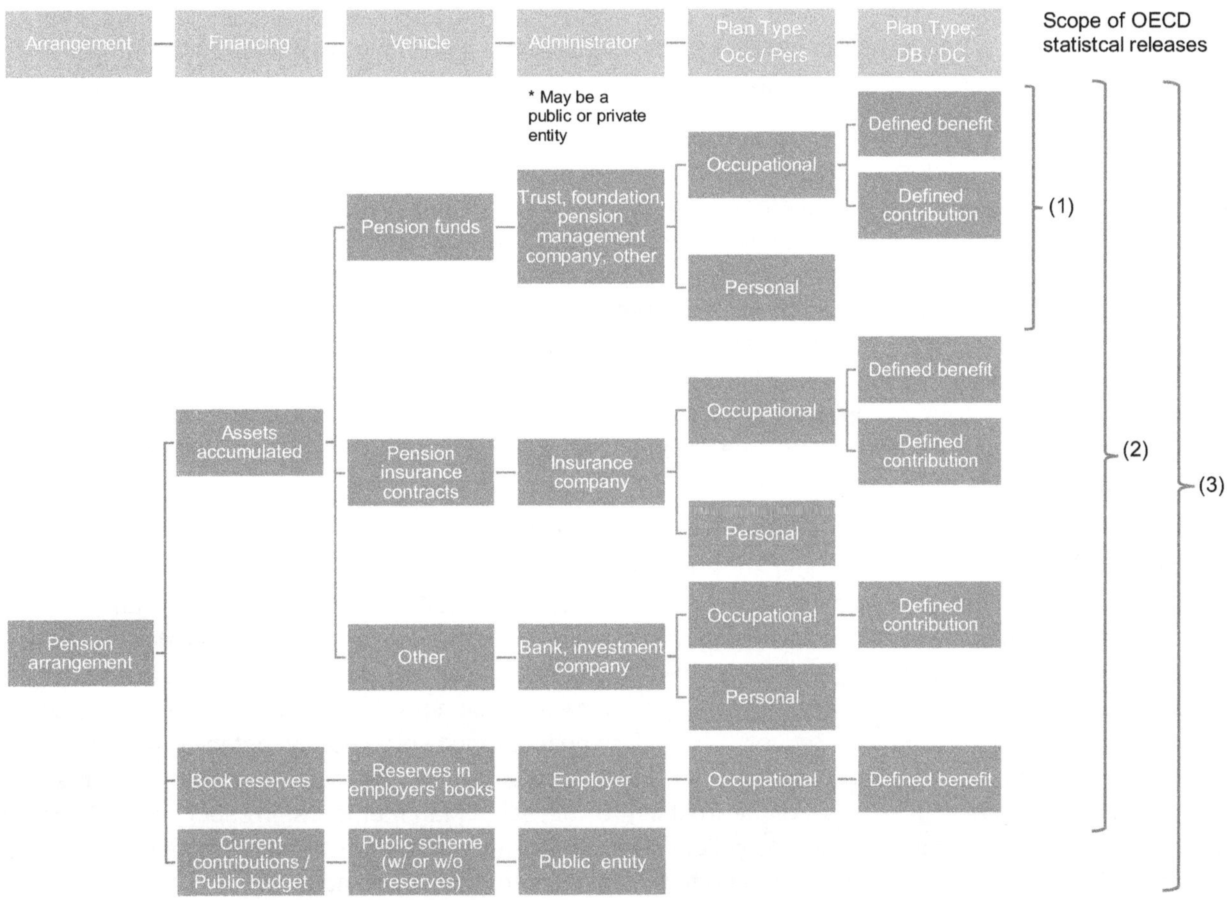

Note: For more details, please see the methodological notes in Annex C.

Pension arrangements are designed to provide benefits to individuals at retirement but finance these benefits in various ways. Benefits can be financed through assets accumulated, through provisions in employers' books, from current contributions or from the public budget.

Members can accrue rights or accumulate assets for their retirement through their contributions or the contributions of their employers during their working lives. These assets are legally separated from the sponsors of the pension plans. Members have a legal or beneficial right or some other contractual claim on these assets.

By contrast, provisions in employers' books are not legally separated from the employers. The accrued pension rights of employees could potentially be at risk if the employers go bankrupt. Some countries where this financing method exists have set up insolvency guarantee schemes (e.g. Germany). Other countries encourage or require employers to purchase credit insurance or arrange equivalent guarantees (e.g. Sweden) to protect the pension rights of employees in the event of employer insolvency.

In most countries, the current contributions that employees and employers pay into public pension arrangements are used to pay the benefits of current retirees (i.e. unfunded or pay-as-you-go (PAYG) plans), while in some others retirement income may be financed by tax revenues (e.g. some social assistance programmes). These arrangements are usually administered by a public institution and may have reserves to cover expenses and smooth benefit payments over time.

Some pension arrangements rely both on current contributions and assets accumulated to finance benefits, such as the earning-related pension plans regulated by the Employees' Pension Act (TyEL) and the Seafarer's Pensions Act (MEL) in Finland. The main part of the pensions in a given year is paid by the contributions received that year. The remaining part is financed by accumulated assets.

Pension plans may be funded through the establishment of pension funds, pension insurance contracts or the purchase of other authorised retirement savings products. Pension funds represent a pool of ring-fenced assets forming an independent legal entity. When pension insurance contracts are used for retirement saving, individuals or their employers pay premiums to insurance companies. Insurance companies manage the assets coming from these premiums (or contributions) together with those coming from their other insurance activities. While the amount of premiums paid for these policies is usually known, it is more difficult to assess the size of assets that insurance companies hold as a result of their pension activities. Individuals or their employers may also open or purchase other retirement savings products offered and administered by banks or investment companies (such as individual retirement accounts (IRAs) in the United States).

Pension funds take different legal forms around the world (Stewart and Yermo, 2008[13]). Pension funds may have a legal personality and capacity in some countries (e.g. Pensionskassen in Austria and Germany, contractual pension funds in Italy, pension funds in the Netherlands and Switzerland). Pension funds in these countries have their own governing board. In some other countries, pension funds are segregated pools of assets without legal personality and capacity. In this case, pension funds are governed and administered by a separate entity. This entity may be a pension fund management company (e.g. in Czechia, Chile, Mexico, the Slovak Republic), a bank or an insurance company for instance. In some other countries (e.g. Ireland, the United Kingdom), the legal form of the pension fund is a trust. The trustees legally own and administer the assets of the trust in the interest of plan members. Irrespective of the legal form of the pension funds, some of the activities, such as those related to the investment of assets or the collection of contributions, may be outsourced to third parties (e.g. asset managers).

Employers (from the public or private sector) may set up a pension plan on behalf of their employees. In such cases, the plan is considered as occupational in the OECD taxonomy.[1] Access to the plan is linked to employment. When individuals choose and set up a plan themselves with a dedicated provider, the plan is personal. Access to certain plans may however be limited to individuals with a professional activity but open to both public and private sector workers (e.g. Mexico). These plans are still considered as personal as individuals independently select material aspects of the plan such as the investment strategy, the fund or the administrator of the fund.

Where the employer is responsible for guaranteeing a benefit or return promise to plan members, the OECD considers such occupational plan as a defined benefit (DB) plan. The benefit promise may be a pension calculated on a number of parameters (e.g. salary, length of employment) or an investment rate of return. In the first case, the plan is considered as DB traditional, while the plan is considered as DB hybrid in the second case. When another party offers a guarantee (e.g. an insurance company), the plan is considered as a protected defined contribution (DC) plan. Otherwise, if there is no (fixed) guarantee, the plan is DC unprotected.

The Global Pension Statistics (GPS) exercise that the OECD carries out in co-operation with the IOPS and the World Bank cover employers' book reserves (which are private pension plans) and all plans accumulating assets, regardless of the financing vehicle and its administrator (public or private institution), the type of plans (occupational, personal, DB or DC) and the type of people covered (public sector workers, private sector workers). Unfunded or pay-as-you-go arrangements with their reserves are out of the scope of this exercise.

This publication mainly relies on all the data collected through this statistical exercise. It endeavours to show data for data for all plans accumulating assets (funded plans) and book reserves, since the 2017 edition of this annual report (scope (2) in Figure A A.1).

Data in the GPS exercise – and therefore in this report – may not always cover book reserves and all plans accumulating assets that exist in each country due to data availability issues. Data are sometimes unavailable ("missing") for a given type of plan in a country (e.g. book reserves in Austria). In other cases, data may be missing only for some plans in a given type of plan. In Ireland for example, two plans qualify as pension insurance contracts according to the OECD taxonomy: retirement annuity contracts and personal retirement savings accounts (PRSAs). Data in the GPS exercise only cover PRSAs. Table A A.1 shows the types of pension plans and book reserves that exist in all the jurisdictions participating in the OECD, IOPS and World Bank statistical exercise. The table also specifies the coverage of the OECD data. More information is available online on the different pension plans in each jurisdiction.[2]

Table A A.1. Existing types of funded pension plans and book reserves by jurisdictions and data coverage of the Global Pension Statistics exercise

	Funded								Book reserves
	Pension funds			Pension insurance contracts			Other		
	Occupational		Personal	Occupational		Personal	Occupational	Personal	
	DB	DC		DB	DC				
OECD countries									
Australia	✓	✓	✓					***Some***	
Austria	***Some***	✓		✓	***Some***	***Some***			Missing
Belgium	✓	✓	***Some***	✓	✓	✓		***Some***	
Canada	✓	✓	***Some***	✓	✓	✓		***Some***	✓
Chile		✓	✓		Missing	Missing	Missing	Missing	
Colombia			✓						
Costa Rica	✓	✓	✓						
Czechia			✓						
Denmark	✓		✓		✓	✓	✓	✓	
Estonia			✓			✓			
Finland	✓			✓		✓			Missing
France	✓	✓	✓	✓	✓	✓			
Germany	✓	✓		Missing	Missing	Missing		Missing	Missing

	Funded								Book reserves
	Pension funds			Pension insurance contracts			Other		
	Occupational		Personal	Occupational		Personal	Occupational	Personal	
	DB	DC		DB	DC				
Greece		✓				Missing			
Hungary		Missing	✓			✓		✓	
Iceland	✓	✓	✓			✓		✓	
Ireland	✓	✓				***Some***		✓	
Israel	✓		✓			Missing		***Some***	
Italy	✓	✓	✓			✓			✓
Japan	✓	✓	✓			✓			✓
Korea				✓	✓	✓	✓	✓	
Latvia		✓	✓					✓	
Lithuania			✓						
Luxembourg	✓	✓			Missing	Missing		Missing	Missing
Mexico	✓	✓	✓	✓	✓	Missing	✓	Missing	
Netherlands	✓	✓		Missing	Missing	Missing			
New Zealand	✓	✓	✓					✓	
Norway	✓			✓	✓	✓			
Poland		✓	✓		✓	✓	✓	✓	
Portugal	✓	✓	✓	Missing	Missing	✓		✓	
Slovak Republic			✓						
Slovenia		✓	✓		✓	✓			
Spain	✓	✓	✓	✓	✓	✓			✓
Sweden	✓	✓	✓	✓	✓	***Some***		✓	***Some***
Switzerland	✓					✓		✓	
Türkiye	Some	✓	✓						✓
United Kingdom	✓	✓		Missing	Missing	Missing			
United States	✓	✓				✓		✓	
Other jurisdictions									
Albania		✓	✓						
Armenia			***Some***						
Botswana		✓	✓						
Brazil	✓	✓				✓			
Bulgaria		✓	✓						
Croatia		✓	✓						
Dominican Republic	✓	***Some***	✓						
Egypt			✓						
Georgia			✓			✓			
Ghana		✓	✓						
Gibraltar				✓	✓	Missing	✓		
Guyana	✓	✓							
Hong Kong (China)	✓	✓		✓	✓				
India	***Some***	✓	✓						
Indonesia	✓	✓	***Some***						
Isle of Man	✓	✓	✓						
Jamaica	✓	✓	✓						
Kazakhstan			✓						
Kenya	✓	✓	✓						
Kosovo*		✓							
Lesotho	✓	✓	Missing						
Liechtenstein	✓	✓							
Macau (China)	✓	✓	✓						

	Funded								Book reserves
	Pension funds			Pension insurance contracts			Other		
	Occupational		Personal	Occupational		Personal	Occupational	Personal	
	DB	DC		DB	DC				
Malawi	✓	✓							
Malaysia	Missing		✓			✓			
Maldives			✓						
Malta		✓	✓			✓			
Mauritius	✓	✓	Missing			Missing			
Morocco		✓							
Mozambique	✓	✓							
Namibia	✓	✓	✓			✓			
Nigeria	✓		✓						
North Macedonia		✓	✓						
Pakistan	Missing	Missing	✓						
Peru			✓						
Romania			✓						
Russia	✓	✓	✓						
Serbia		✓	✓						
South Africa	✓	✓	✓				✓	✓	
Suriname	✓	✓			Missing	Missing			
Tanzania	***Some***		✓						
Thailand		***Some***	Missing						
Uganda	✓	✓	✓						
Ukraine			✓						
Uruguay			✓						
Zambia	***Some***	✓	Missing			Missing			
Zimbabwe	***Some***	✓	Missing			Missing			

Note: "DB": defined benefit; "DC": defined contribution. This Table gives the data coverage of this report, based on the OECD/IOPS/World Bank Global Pension Statistics (GPS) exercise. When a cell is grey with a tick, this means that the GPS exercise covers all the plans of this type for a given country. "Some" means that the GPS exercise only covers some plans of this type. "Missing" means that this type of plan exists but the OECD data do not cover it. Data for Australia cover the whole superannuation sector except retirement savings accounts (RSAs). Data for Germany refer to Pensionskassen and Pensionsfonds only. In Hungary, there is one institution for occupational retirement provision but its market share is negligible compared to other pension providers administering personal pension plans. In Norway, since 2021, members of DC schemes can consolidate their previous DC savings and contributions from their current job into a single account (own pension account). See Annex B for a full and detailed description of all types of funded plans and book reserves in the jurisdictions participating in the OECD/IOPS/World Bank Global Pension Statistics exercise. Any deviation to this data coverage in this report is reported in the specific notes of the related Table or Figure.

StatLink https://stat.link/7vhi5f

This edition of *Pension Markers in Focus* has a broader coverage of asset-backed pension systems than before, by incorporating reserves of public PAYG pension arrangements in the OECD area (scope (3) in Figure A A.1). Data on these public reserves mainly come from the website of the public pension reserve funds managing these reserves and from desk research.

Notes

[1] The definitions of pension plans by the OECD's Working Party on Private Pensions are available in the publication *Private Pensions: OECD Classification and Glossary*, available at https://www.oecd.org/daf/fin/private-pensions/privatepensionsoecdclassificationandglossary.htm.

[2] See https://www.oecd.org/pensions/private-pensions/pensionmarketsinfocus.htm

Annex B. Statistical annex

Table A B.1. Additional statistical tables

Table B.1. Total assets in pension plans, in millions of national currency, 2001-2022
Table B.2. Total assets in pension plans, in USD million, 2001-2022
Table B.3. Total assets in pension plans, as a % of GDP, 2001-2022
Table B.4. Contributions into pension plans, 2001-2022
Table B.5. Pension benefit flows, 2001-2022
Table B.6. Annual nominal investment rates of return of pension plans, 2002-2022
Table B.7. Annual real investment rates of return of pension plans, 2002-2022
Table B.8. Allocation of assets in pension plans in equities, 2001-2022
Table B.9. Allocation of assets in pension plans in bills and bonds, 2001-2022
Table B.10. Allocation of assets in pension plans in cash and deposits, 2001-2022
Table B.11. Allocation of assets in pension plans in the "other" category, 2001-2022
Table B.12. Share of assets in pension plans invested abroad, 2001-2022
Table B.13. Evolution in the participation rate, by type of plan and by jurisdiction

StatLink https://stat.link/isy8dh

Table A B.2. Overview of asset-backed pension systems

Table B.14. Coverage of the OECD Global Pension Statistics exercise

StatLink https://stat.link/x0ieuw

Annex C. Methodological notes

Pension authorities and other bodies provided the primary source material for this report, as part of the OECD/IOPS/ World Bank Global Pension Statistics (GPS) exercise. Data come from official administrative sources and are revised on an ongoing basis so as to better reflect the most recent figures for every past year. Some divergences may exist between national reporting standards and the compilation method of certain data for the GPS exercise. For this reason, data providers are regularly requested to provide methodological information relevant for developing a thorough understanding of their submission under the GPS framework. The general and specific methodological notes below provide some explanations in this respect.

General notes

- Conventional signs: ".." means not available. "|" means methodological break in series.
- This report is mainly based on the answers of pension authorities and other bodies to an annual data request. Some statistics for some jurisdictions come from publicly available reports, databases or websites of other national or international organisations: Japan (Bank of Japan) and Switzerland (Federal Social Insurance Office's publication *Statistique des assurances sociales suisses* for personal plans) among OECD countries; and Argentina (International Association of Pension Fund Supervisors (AIOS)), Bolivia (AIOS), China (People's Republic of) (Ministry of Human Resources and Social Security (MOHRSS)), Croatia (website of the Croatian Financial Services Supervisory Agency (HANFA) before 2014), the Dominican Republic (AIOS before 2014), El Salvador (AIOS), India (annual reports of the Employees' Provident Fund Organisation for Employees' Provident Fund, Employees' Pension Scheme and Employees' Deposit Linked Insurance Scheme), Panama (AIOS) and Uruguay (AIOS before 2016) among non-OECD jurisdictions.
- Data on stock variables refer to the end of the year while data on flow variables are provided over the whole year in the report. The reference period is the calendar year, except for: Australia where the reference period is the financial year ending in June; India where the reference period ends in March of the following year for Employees' Provident Fund, Employees' Pension Scheme and Employees' Deposit Linked Insurance Scheme; and New Zealand (until 2014). Data for New Zealand up to 2013 are based on a 31 March balance date for most of the schemes.
- Data on defined benefit plans in Ireland include one large scheme in which members build up rights on a defined contribution basis but which is subject to the Irish funding standard because there is an option for members to purchase an annuity from the scheme at retirement.
- Slovenia adopted the euro in 2007, the Slovak Republic in 2009, Estonia in 2011, Latvia in 2014 and Lithuania in 2015. The whole time series (in millions of national currency) are expressed in millions of euro for these countries (even before their adoption of the euro). Data in national currency for Croatia are expressed in kuna even if the euro became the official currency of Croatia as of January 2023.

- This report uses five main additional reference series: exchange rates to convert values in US dollars, GDP, the variation of the consumer price index (CPI), population and average annual wages:
  - This report uses end-of-period exchange rates for all variables valued at the end of the year, and period-average rates for variables representing a flow over the year. These rates come from the IMF International Financial Statistics database.
  - GDP values for OECD countries are extracted from the OECD Annual National Accounts and Quarterly National Accounts databases. GDP values for non-OECD jurisdictions come from the IMF World Economic Outlook released in April 2023, except for Gibraltar (Abstract of Statistics 2015 of the Statistics Office of Gibraltar), Isle of Man (the National Income webpage of the Official Isle of Man Government website) and Liechtenstein (UN National Accounts Main Aggregates Database).
  - Consumer price indices are from the OECD Main Economic Indicators database for OECD countries in most cases, and from the IMF International Financial Statistics database for Costa Rica (2022), Japan (2021, 2022) and for all non-OECD jurisdictions except for Gibraltar (Abstract of Statistics 2015 of the Statistics Office of Gibraltar), Kazakhstan in 2022 (Bureau of National Statistics) and Papua New Guinea (World Bank Consumer Price Index database).
  - Data on population are from the OECD Labour Force Statistics database for OECD countries and from the World Bank World Development Indicators for all the other jurisdictions.

Specific notes

Figure 1.1:

The "Other" category includes loans, land and buildings, unallocated insurance contracts, hedge funds, private equity funds, structured products, other mutual funds (i.e. not invested in equities, bills and bonds or cash and deposits) and other investments. Negative values (due to derivatives) have been excluded from the calculations of the allocation of pension assets. The Global Pension Statistics exercise gathers information on investments of pension plan assets in collective investment schemes (CIS) and the look-through of these investments in equities, bills and bonds, cash and deposits and other. Data on asset allocation in this Figure include both direct investments in equities, bills and bonds, cash and deposits and indirect investments through CIS when the look-through of CIS investments is available. In such case, the Figure shows the overall exposure of pension plan assets in the selected asset classes. When the look-through is not available, the Figure only shows the direct investments of pension plan assets in equities, bills and bonds, cash and deposits and other assets, and investments in collective investment schemes are shown in a separate category. Data are as at end-June 2021 for Australia and New Zealand Superannuation Fund, March 2022 for Canada's CPP reserves.

Figure 1.2:

The charts are based on the annual investment rates of return reported in the statistical annex of the report (Annex B). Please refer to the notes of this statistical annex for more country or fund-specific notes. The annual returns are calculated over the period Dec 2021-Dec 2022 except for Australia (June 2021-June 2022), Canada's CPP reserves (March 2022-March 2023), Japan's GPIF (March 2022-March 2023), New Zealand Superannuation Fund (June 2021-June 2022).

Table 1.1:

The last 5, 10, 15 and 20-year annual averages are calculated over the periods Dec 2017-Dec 2022, Dec 2012-Dec 2022, Dec 2007-Dec 2022 and Dec 2002-Dec 2022 respectively, except for Australia (starting and ending in June), Canada's CPP reserves (starting and ending in March of the following year), Japan's

GPIF (starting and ending in March of the following year), and New Zealand Superannuation Fund (starting and ending in June).

Figure 1.3:

The charts show the change in the proportion of assets invested in equities (x-axis) and bonds (y-axis) between end-2021 and end-2022 for pension plans in 35 OECD countries (dark blue dots) and 38 other non-OECD jurisdictions (light blue dots), and for 20 public pension reserve funds in the OECD area (grey dots). For readability purposes, the first chart does not show Türkiye (where investments in equity increased by 6.5 percentage points (pp) while investments in bonds declined by 25.4 pp) nor Georgia (+7.3 pp in equity, +27.4 pp in bonds). The simple average is calculated on all reporting OECD and non-OECD jurisdictions (first chart), and on all public pension reserve funds with available data (second chart).

Figure 2.2:

Participation rates are provided with respect to the total working-age population (i.e. individuals aged 15 to 64 years old), except for Ireland (workers aged between 20 and 69).

Data on personal plans for Austria refer to PZV contracts. In Estonia, participation in the second pillar is still mandatory for people born on 1 January 1983 or later, but they can apply for an exemption from making contributions. Persons who opt out do still have account opened, but they are not counted in the data on second pillar members. Data for Hungary refer to pension fund members only. Data for Israel refer to new and general pension funds. For Italy, the coverage rate that is shown under voluntary occupational plans also covers individuals automatically enrolled in a plan. Data on mandatory plans for Norway refer to private and municipal group pensions. Data on voluntary personal plans in Poland refer to members in open pension funds. Data for the Slovak Republic refer to the second pension pillar only.

Figure 2.3:

The high growth of contributions paid in Angola in 2022 relates to the closed pension fund of Banco Nacional de Angola. Data for Mexico refer to personal pension plans only. Data for Georgia refer to the second pension pillar only.

Figure 3.1:

The chart shows the amount of assets at the end of each year, from end-2001 to end-2022, based on annual data. The total amounts of assets at the end of a given year are calculated on all the jurisdictions for which a value is available. The number of jurisdictions that the totals include may therefore vary over the years. Totals are expressed in current prices.

Figure 3.2:

The size of the rectangles for pension plans is proportional to the amount of assets in jurisdictions within the same area (e.g. OECD), but not with pension plans in jurisdictions outside this area. Similarly, the size of the rectangles for public reserves is proportional to the amount of public reserves within the same aera but is not comparable with the size of pension plans. The "Other OECD" does not include Belgium for which the amount of assets in asset-backed pension plans (excluding reserves of unfunded/PAYG plans) is unavailable yet for 2022. The "Other non-OECD" category includes the following reporting jurisdictions: Albania, Angola, Armenia, Botswana, Bulgaria, Croatia, Dominican Republic, Egypt, Georgia, Ghana, Guyana, Indonesia, Isle of Man, Jamaica, Kazakhstan, Kenya, Kosovo*, Lesotho, Liechtenstein, Macau (China), Malaysia, Maldives, Malta, Mauritius, Morocco, Namibia, Nigeria, North Macedonia, Pakistan, Peru, Romania, Serbia, Suriname, Uruguay, Zambia, Zimbabwe.

* This designation is without prejudice to positions on status, and is in line with United Nations Security Council Resolution 1244/99 and the Advisory Opinion of the International Court of Justice on Kosovo's declaration of independence.

Figure 3.3:

Data for Canada refer to trusteed pension funds only. Data for Georgia refer to the second pension pillar only.

Figure 3.5:

Benefits and transfers are for payments for retirement. Data for Finland refer to pension funds only. Data for Croatia refer to pension funds in charge of the accumulation phase and do not include contributions nor payments from pension insurance companies in charge of the pay-out phase. Data for Hong Kong (China) refer to MPF schemes only.

Figure 3.6:

Benefits and transfers are for payments for retirement. Data for Austria refer to Pensionskassen only. Data for Canada, Finland, Hungary, Norway, Spain and Switzerland refer to pension funds only. Data for Denmark refer to benefits paid by pension funds and pension insurance contracts only. Data for Estonia refer to benefits paid by 2nd pension pillar plans only. Data for Italy refer to benefits paid from pension funds and book reserves only. Data for Türkiye refer to personal pension plans only. Data for Croatia refer to benefit payments and asset transfers from pension funds in charge of the accumulation phase. Data for Hong Kong (China) refer to MPF schemes only.

Figure 4.1:

The chart shows the evolution of the liabilities (measured by the net technical provisions) of defined benefit (DB) plans at the end of each year. All liabilities of DB plans (instead of technical provisions only) are considered for Ireland and the United States. Data for Finland refer to DB plans in pension funds only. Data for Luxembourg refer to DB traditional plans under the supervision of the CSSF. Data for the Netherlands and Switzerland include all types of pension funds. Data for the United Kingdom come from the Purple Book 2022 published by the Pension Protection Fund and show the liabilities valued on an s179 basis (instead of net technical provisions). Liabilities for Hong Kong (China) refer to the amount of aggregated past service liability in DB ORSO schemes.

Figure 4.2:

The chart shows the funding ratio of defined benefit (DB) plans at end-2021 and end-2022, and the difference in values between the two dates. This difference is expressed in percentage points (pp) and is shown in red (respectively green) when the funding ratio declined (resp. increased) between end-2021 and end-2022. The funding ratio is calculated as the ratio of total investment and net technical provisions for DB plans managed by pension funds using values reported by national authorities in the OECD questionnaire. All liabilities of DB plans (instead of technical provisions only) are considered for Ireland and the United States. Data for Finland refer to DB plans in pension funds only. Data for Luxembourg refer to DB traditional plans under the supervision of the CSSF. Data for the Netherlands and Switzerland include all types of pension funds. Data for the United Kingdom come from the Purple Book 2022 published by the Pension Protection Fund and show the ratio of assets and liabilities valued on an s179 basis (instead of net technical provisions). The 10.3 pp increase in the funding ratio of DB plans in the United Kingdom comes from market movements (6 pp), the new s179 basis from May 2021 (2.6 pp) and a change in the universe of DB plans (1.7 pp). Liabilities for Hong Kong (China) refer to the amount of aggregated past service liability in DB ORSO schemes.

Table 5.2:

"x" means that the type of fee does not exist or is not allowed in the country. All the fees are expressed in this Table as a percentage of total assets, even when fees are levied on salaries, contributions or investment income. These percentages are therefore not comparable with the maximum set by law when this maximum is expressed as a percentage of salaries, contributions or investment income. (1) Data refer to June 2022 for entities with more than six members and come from APRA Annual Superannuation Bulletin. (2) Fees are charged on qualifying income. Severance fund management fees are not included. (3) Data refer to the ROP only. (4) Data refer to voluntary private pension funds only. (5) Data refer to personal plans only. (6) Data refer to open pension funds only.

Figure A A.1:

(1) Scope of the note *Pension Funds in Figures* (renamed *Pension Markets in Focus - Preliminary data on pension funds*) until 2022; and scope of the full report *Pension Markets in Focus* before the 2017 edition. (2) Scope of the OECD Global Pension Statistics exercise; scope of the note *Pension Markets in Focus - Preliminary data* since 2023; scope the full report *Pension Markets in Focus* since the 2017 edition until 2022. (3) Scope of this 2023 edition of *Pension Markets in Focus*.

www.ingramcontent.com/pod-product-compliance
Lightning Source LLC
Chambersburg PA
CBHW061225240926
51846CB00006B/1362
* 9 7 8 9 2 6 4 4 4 4 2 3 2 *